Federal Vision

heresy at the root

DAVID J. ENGELSMA

Federal Vision

heresy at the root

Reformed Free Publishing Association
Jenison, Michigan

Reformed Free Publishing Association
1894 Georgetown Center Drive
Jenison, Michigan 49428-7137
Phone: 616.457.5970
Fax: 616.457.5980
www.rfpa.org
mail@rfpa.org

The Reformed Free Publishing Association gratefully
acknowledges the support of Covenant Protestant Reformed
Church, Ballymena, Northern Ireland, and the evangelism
committees of Crete Protestant Reformed Church, Crete, Illinois,
and Southwest Protestant Reformed Church, Wyoming, Michigan,
in partial payment for the production costs of this book.

Book design by Erika Kiel

ISBN: 978-1-936054-07-7
LCCN: 2011945402

In thankful acknowledgment of the work of my theological and spiritual ancestors, Hendrik de Cock, Simon van Velzen, and Hendrik Joffers, on behalf of God's covenant of sovereign grace. Some "fathers" and all stalwarts of the Secession of 1834 in the Netherlands, they preached the truth, contended for the faith, suffered for their witness (at the hands of enemies within, as well as enemies without), and gave God the glory.

THEY LED THE WAY

They are not forgotten

CONTENTS

PREFACE

The first part of this book is an expanded version of a speech commemorating the sixteenth-century Reformation of the church.

Commemoration of the Reformation by Protestant churches becomes a rarity in the twenty-first century. In a time when Protestant churches are deep in ecumenical relations with the Roman Catholic Church, the Reformation and its gospel of salvation by grace alone are an embarrassment to Protestants.

Where the Reformation is still observed, there is the danger that the commemoration is hypocritical. In the language Jesus used in exposing such hypocrisy on the part of the church officials of his day, Protestant churches build the tomb of Martin Luther and garnish the sepulcher of John Calvin. However, in reality they are the theological and spiritual children of those who hated and opposed the reformers (Matt. 23:29–31), for the Protestant churches confess, or tolerate, another gospel than the gospel of the Reformation. It is the false gospel of a grace of God dependent on the will of the sinner; of a justification of the sinner that takes into account the sinner's own obedience; and of a salvation conditioned by the sinner's works.

Genuine commemoration of the Reformation consists of maintaining the Reformation's confession of the one, true gospel of salvation by sovereign grace.

It consists also of anathematizing—cursing in the name of God—the false gospel of the works, will, and worth of the sinner, that is, the false gospel of a conditional, resistible grace and a conditional, losable salvation, as well as those who preach it. "If any man preach any other gospel unto you than that ye have received, let him be accursed" (Gal. 1:9).

Especially is the church that is truly the heir of Christ's work in the Reformation called to expose and condemn the false gospel in its contemporary form.

Hence this book: *Federal Vision*.

The theology that calls itself the federal vision is a grave threat, if not the *chief* threat, to the Reformed faith—the Reformation's gospel of grace—in our time. The heretical fruit of this theology is the bold teaching of justification by faith and works. Its heretical root is the doctrine of a conditional covenant.

Some avowed opponents of the federal vision busy themselves with the fruit. None touches the root—with the proverbial ten-foot pole. Their efforts, therefore, are vain and deceiving.

This book purposes the eradication of the heresy of the federal vision.

Hence the subtitle: *Heresy at the Root*.

This uprooting of the heretical doctrine of the federal vision ardently desires the planting in Reformed and Presbyterian churches, or replanting, as the case may be, of the truth of the unconditional covenant. This truth is the gospel of the Reformation. Only this truth moves covenant children to keep God's commandments out of love for him. Only this truth gives assurance of salvation to the baptized children of believers, old and young. Only this truth gives God the glory for covenant salvation.

The second section of the book consists of answers to questions concerning the federal vision and the covenant from the audience at the Reformation Day lecture. These questions with their answers shed light on the great covenant controversy of our day.

PART 1

Eradicating the Federal Vision

INTRODUCTION TO THE
FEDERAL VISION CONTROVERSY

1

The Coming of the Vision | A Heretical Vision
A Real and Present Danger

The federal vision is a theology—a body of teachings—within the conservative Reformed and Presbyterian churches in North America. This theology denies all the doctrines of sovereign grace, centering on justification by faith alone. As all the world knows, the truth of justification by faith alone was the heart of the sixteenth-century Reformation of the church. As Romans and Galatians teach, as all the reformers testified, and as all the Reformation creeds confess, justification by faith alone is the heart of the gospel. The federal vision, therefore, denies the heart of the gospel.

The federal vision is favorable to, and closely allied with, the new perspective on Paul. This exegetical and doctrinal movement dismisses as mistaken the Reformation's understanding of the gospel as taught especially in Romans and Galatians. It is, therefore, a movement that at one stroke annihilates all the Reformation creeds, from the Heidelberg Catechism to the Westminster Confession of Faith. All the Reformed and Presbyterian confessions express as gospel truth the Reformation's understanding of the gospel, especially in Romans and Galatians.

The fascination with and dependence on the new perspective on Paul on the part of the federal vision are evident in all its proponents. Rich Lusk boldly shoved the federal vision's basic agreement with the new perspective on Paul in the faces of all the theologians at the Knox Theological Seminary Colloquium on the federal vision. This was a high-powered conference of advocates and critics of the federal vision in 2003.

At this conference, having criticized the reformers for their erroneous understanding of Paul's condemnation of those who taught justification by works of the law, Lusk explained Galatians 3 and 4. Contrary to the Reformation, "Paul was not battling legalism" in these chapters. Rather, the apostle was opposing Jewish teachers who "were suggesting submission to the old covenant identity badges as the way of entrance into the true people of God." Everyone in the least familiar with the new perspective on Paul immediately recognizes the new perspective lingo and line. Lest anyone at the colloquium fail to notice that he was parroting the new perspective line, Lusk referred the theologians in attendance to a book by N. T. Wright—new perspective darling of the men of the federal vision—"for complete exegesis."[1]

The federal vision is furthered by a widespread and aggressive promotion of "biblical theology" at the expense of "systematic theology." The contemporary promotion of "biblical theology" is a thinly disguised attack on the Reformed and Presbyterian creeds, especially the Canons of Dordt and the Westminster Confession of Faith. The attack on the creeds in the name of "biblical theology" becomes increasingly open and bold. Federal vision theologian Don Garlington has recently savaged the Canons of Dordt: "The 'five points' [of Calvinism]...are schematized and tend to be artificial, as...based on a systematic rather than a biblical theology."[2]

Since the struggle of orthodoxy with the Arminian heresy at Dordt in the early seventeenth century, the federal vision is one of the most deadly threats to the gospel of grace that Christ restored to the church by the sixteenth-century Reformation.

---

1 Rich Lusk, "A Response to 'The Biblical Plan of Salvation,'" in *The Auburn Avenue Theology, Pros & Cons: Debating the Federal Vision*, ed. E. Calvin Beisner (Fort Lauderdale, FL: Knox Theological Seminary, 2004), 132–33.

2 Don Garlington, "Covenantal Nomism and the Exile," in *A Faith That Is Never Alone: A Response to Westminster Seminary California*, ed. P. Andrew Sandlin (La Grange, CA: Kerygma Press, 2007), 391.

THE COMING OF THE VISION

Briefly, the historical background of the theology and movement within conservative Reformed and Presbyterian churches in North America that calls itself the federal vision is this. In 2000, Norman Shepherd published a book titled *The Call of Grace*.[3] The subtitle is significant, indicating that the book advocates and defends a certain doctrine of the covenant: *How the Covenant Illuminates Salvation and Evangelism*.

At the time he published the book, Shepherd was a minister in the Christian Reformed Church. Earlier, for much of his career, he had been a theologian in the Orthodox Presbyterian Church, teaching systematic theology in Westminster Seminary (Philadelphia) for eighteen years.

In the book Shepherd openly and explicitly attacks all the doctrines of sovereign grace confessed by the Reformed churches in the three forms of unity and in the Westminster standards. On the foreground in the book, although not at the heart of it, is the denial of justification by faith alone, altogether apart from any good work of the believer.[4]

The publication of Shepherd's book brought to light the reprehensible handling of Shepherd and his heresies by the faculty and board of Westminster Seminary (Philadelphia) and by the ecclesiastical assemblies of the Orthodox Presbyterian Church in the late 1970s and early 1980s, while Shepherd was dogmatics professor at Westminster Seminary. This shameful history was kept hidden until Shepherd's publication of his book made the suppression impossible. Westminster Seminary and a presbytery of the Orthodox Presbyterian Church handled Shepherd and his teachings by approving the teachings and by exonerating and protecting Shepherd.[5]

---

3 Norman Shepherd, *The Call of Grace: How the Covenant Illuminates Salvation and Evangelism* (Phillipsburg, NJ: P&R, 2000).

4 For demonstration of these observations, see David J. Engelsma, *The Covenant of God and the Children of Believers: Sovereign Grace in the Covenant* (Grandville, MI: Reformed Free Publishing Association, 2005), 133–232.

5 For this history see O. Palmer Robertson, *The Current Justification Controversy* (Unicoi, TN: Trinity Foundation, 2003); A. Donald MacLeod, "A

The publication of Shepherd's book also occasioned the opening of the floodgates of public defense of Shepherd's teachings and aggressive promotion of them within many of the reputedly conservative Reformed and Presbyterian denominations in North America, including the Orthodox Presbyterian Church, the Presbyterian Church in America, and the United Reformed Churches.

The publication of *The Call of Grace* was the birth of the federal vision. The result of the book has been a spate of writings in books and periodicals; high-level colloquiums; conferences; official church decisions on concrete cases; reports of study committees; and, it is reported, endless discussions on the Internet.

Virtually all the conservative Reformed churches have had to concern themselves with the federal vision.

The advocates of the doctrines published by Shepherd call their distinctive theology federal vision. One thing about this name should be noted, the main thing: derived from the Latin *foedus*, "federal" means covenant.

A HERETICAL VISION

The federal vision is a heresy. It is a stubborn, persistent, deliberate departure from and denial of a cardinal truth of Scripture, as this truth is rightly and authoritatively summarized and systematized in the Reformed creeds. Specifically, the federal vision is heretical in the doctrine that it puts on the foreground: justification by faith and works. By this doctrine the federal vision denies justification by faith alone.

Already in 1976, it now comes out, Shepherd informed the authorities at Westminster Seminary that he taught that "to insist

Painful Parting, 1977–1983: Justifying Justification," in *W. Stanford Reid: An Evangelical Calvinist in the Academy* (Montreal: McGill-Queen's University Press, 2004), 257–79; Paul M. Elliott, *Christianity and Neo-Liberalism: The Spiritual Crisis in the Orthodox Presbyterian Church and Beyond* (Unicoi, TN: Trinity Foundation, 2005); and W. Robert Godfrey, "Westminster Seminary, the Doctrine of Justification, and the Reformed Confessions," in *The Pattern of Sound Doctrine: Systematic Theology at the Westminster Seminaries*, ed. David van Drunen (Phillipsburg, NJ: P&R, 2004), 127–48.

on faith alone for justification is a serious impoverishment."[6] Shepherd added that it is possible to lose the grace of justification and that justification can increase and decrease.[7] These teachings are implications of the false doctrine of justification by works. The righteousness of Christ, imputed to the elect sinner by faith alone, does not increase or decrease. It cannot be lost.

The federal vision's teaching concerning justification is the doctrine of the Roman Catholic Church, condemned by the Reformation. It is the doctrine of justification by works that Scripture condemns in Romans 3–5 and in the epistle to the Galatians. "Therefore we conclude that a man is justified by faith without the deeds of the law" (Rom. 3:28). "No man is justified by the law in the sight of God...for, the just shall live by faith" (Gal. 3:11).

The federal vision's doctrine of justification flatly contradicts question and answer 60 of the Heidelberg Catechism: "How art thou righteous before God? Only by true faith in Jesus Christ."[8] It contradicts question and answer 62 of the Catechism as well:

> But why can not our good works be the whole or part of our righteousness before God?

> Because the righteousness which can stand before the judgment-seat of God must be perfect throughout, and wholly conformable to the divine law; whereas even our best works in this life are all imperfect and defiled with sin.[9]

The federal vision's doctrine of justification by faith and works is the rejection of the sixteenth-century Reformation of the church at its heart. It is the denial of the gospel of grace at its heart.

6 Martin Downes, *Risking the Truth: Handling Error in the Church* (Fearn, Rosshire, Scotland: Christian Focus, 2009), 137.

7 Ibid.

8 Heidelberg Catechism, Q&A 60, in *Creeds of Christendom with a History and Critical Notes*, 6th ed., 3 vols., ed. Philip Schaff (New York: Harper and Row, 1931; repr., Grand Rapids, MI: Baker, 2007), 3:326.

9 Heidelberg Catechism, Q&A 62, in ibid., 3:327.

Since justification by faith alone is the heart of the gospel, the men of the federal vision also, necessarily, deny *all* the doctrines of grace as confessed by the Reformed believer in the three forms of unity and in the Westminster standards: sovereign, eternal predestination as the source of all salvation; limited, efficacious atonement as the basis of all salvation; irresistible grace as the power of all salvation; and the preservation of saints as the benefit and comfort of gracious salvation.

The federal vision denies all these doctrines of grace *openly and explicitly.*

The federal vision is heresy—gross heresy.

A REAL AND PRESENT DANGER

The threat of the federal vision to Reformed and Presbyterian believers and their children has not diminished in the slightest in the past ten years or so since Shepherd published *The Call of Grace.* On the contrary, the danger to Reformed churches and church members is greater today than ever before.

Some might suppose that the danger has lessened, indeed, passed altogether. There are ministers and theologians in the churches who would very much like to convince the members that there is no longer a danger. Their reason for supposing or contending that the danger has passed is that some prominent theologians have condemned the federal vision's teaching of justification by works. Some Reformed churches have adopted reports affirming justification by faith alone in opposition to the federal vision.

"All is well once again!" "We have resisted the error!"

But the notion that there is no longer any danger is a mistake. The mistake is fatal to the churches where it lodges. The danger of the federal vision remains. It is the more dangerous because now, supposedly overcome, it is being ignored.

The federal vision remains a danger, first, because prominent, influential men in the Reformed churches continue to defend and promote the theology of the federal vision. There is Shepherd who, although a member of the Christian Reformed Church, exercises great influence upon many in the Orthodox

Presbyterian Church, the Presbyterian Church in America, the United Reformed Churches, and other denominations. There is the Orthodox Presbyterian theologian Richard B. Gaffin Jr. who vigorously defended Shepherd's theology for seven years at Westminster Seminary and before the assemblies of the Orthodox Presbyterian Church, praised Shepherd's *The Call of Grace* as "valuable instruction on what it means to live in covenant with God" and as beneficial to "anyone concerned about biblical growth in Christian life and witness," and has risen to the defense of the theology of the federal vision when it has been called into question before the assemblies of the Orthodox Presbyterian Church.[10]

There is John Frame, professor of theology in the Presbyterian Church in America, who also defended Shepherd during the controversy over Shepherd's theology at Westminster Seminary. Incapable of rousing himself to holy anger over the denial of justification by faith alone, Frame has, however, vented unholy rage against all those who criticize the federal vision as heretical, calling the critics "stupid, irresponsible, and divisive."[11]

10   On Gaffin's powerful role in defending Shepherd and his doctrine, see Robertson, *The Current Justification Controversy*; Elliott, *Christianity and Neo-Liberalism*; and John W. Robbins, *A Companion to the Current Justification Controversy* (Unicoi, TN: Trinity Foundation, 2003). For Gaffin's hearty recommendation of Shepherd's *The Call of Grace*, see the back cover of *The Call of Grace*. For Gaffin's later spirited defense of a proponent of the federal vision before the general assembly of the Orthodox Presbyterian Church, see Elliott, "The Kinnaird Case and Its Aftermath," in *Christianity and Neo-Liberalism*, 175–237.

11   On Frame's defense of Shepherd, see Elliott, *Christianity and Neo-Liberalism*, 130. For Frame's angry denunciation of criticism of the federal vision, see foreword, in *Backbone of the Bible: Covenant in Contemporary Perspective*, ed. P. Andrew Sandlin (Nacogdoches, TX: Covenant Media Press, 2004), xii. To this denunciation, Frame added, "Theological professors who make such comments [criticizing the federal vision as heresy]...do not have the intellectual, theological, or spiritual maturity to prepare students for gospel ministers." The truth is that any professor of theology in a Reformed seminary who will *not* condemn the federal vision as heresy ought to be deposed from office as unfaithful to his sacred calling. This calling includes cautioning his students "in regard to the errors and heresies of the old, but especially of the new day" (Form for the Installation of Professors of Theology, in *The Confessions and the Church Order of the Protestant Reformed Churches* [Grandville, MI: Protestant

There are the board and faculty of Westminster Seminary, who defended Shepherd to the end. They have never confessed their sins of approving the doctrine of justification by faith and works and of unleashing the federal vision upon the Reformed and Presbyterian churches in North America by releasing Professor Shepherd with a good testimonial.

There are the hundreds of pastors, professors, and missionaries trained by Professor Shepherd, Professor Gaffin, and other likeminded Westminster Seminary professors in the theology of the federal vision.

There is the peripatetic independent Steve Schlissel, who spreads the covenant theology of the federal vision to the ends of the earth.

There is the popular Douglas Wilson with all his zealous Christian reconstructionist colleagues, within and without Wilson's Confederation of Reformed Evangelical Churches.

Second, and even more importantly, the federal vision remains a danger because with the exception of the radical criticism of the federal vision by the Protestant Reformed Churches (that falls on deaf ears), no Reformed theologian, denomination, or study committee report has taken hold of the federal vision *at its root*. None has so much as addressed the root of the heresy.

The denial of justification by faith alone and, with this fundamental gospel truth, *all* the doctrines of grace is only the bad fruit of the theology of the federal vision. It is not the root of the federal vision. Some critics have lopped off the bitter fruit—the denial of justification by faith alone—but all have left the root, whence this fruit grows, strictly alone. All have refused to touch the root.

And this makes all the criticism of the federal vision, and what mild condemnation of it there has been—"error" not heresy— an exercise in futility. Indeed, such criticism of the federal

Reformed Churches in America], 297); "vindicat[ing] sound doctrine against heresies and errors" (Church Order of Dordt, Art. 18, in ibid, 386); and refuting and contradicting all errors that militate against the doctrines of the three forms of unity, "particularly those which were condemned by the [Synod of Dordt]," namely, Arminianism (Formula of Subscription, in ibid, 326).

vision renders the heresy all the more dangerous, because the members of the churches are deluded into thinking that the evil has been eradicated when, in fact, it remains untouched in its pernicious root.

The obvious example that is readily understood by everyone is cancer in the physical body. What doctor is satisfied with cutting off the external lumps, while neglecting to get at the malignant tumor deep within, and then assuring the anxious patient, "You are healed; all is well"? And what cancer patient goes home in peace, knowing that such malpractice was his treatment?

There is a cancer in the body of the Reformed and Presbyterian churches. It is seated deep in the body. By this time it has spread its tentacles widely. Denial of justification by faith alone is a manifestation of the cancer—a symptom—bad enough, alarming to be sure, but only the fruit, not the root, of the deadly evil.

In this book, in love for the Reformed faith, in love for the Reformed churches, in love for the members of the Reformed and Presbyterian churches, and in love for Jesus Christ, whose faith and church they are, but also in hatred of the lie that corrupts the gospel of grace and of those who deliberately and stubbornly teach the lie, I expose the root of the federal vision.

I intend to destroy it.

THE DEVELOPMENT OF A
CONDITIONAL COVENANT

2

The Distinctive Covenant Doctrine of the Federal Vision
Origins of the Conditional Covenant

The federal vision is a theology of the covenant—a body of
teachings about the covenant. This is what the federal vision
is fundamentally. Only secondarily is it a doctrine of justification,
of predestination, of sanctification, and of perseverance. All
of the controversial teachings of the federal vision regarding a
salvation that is dependent upon man's own works stand or fall
with its covenant doctrine.

That the federal vision is essentially a doctrine of the
covenant, the movement itself declares by its name. "Federal"
means covenant. The federal vision is a distinctive doctrine of
the covenant of God with his people in Jesus Christ.

About this covenant in Christ, the federal vision is a vision,
according to its proponents. By "vision" in the name of their theology, the men of the federal vision propose that their covenant
doctrine is new and different. It is certainly new and strange
in comparison with the covenant doctrine of the Reformed
creeds. This is evident from the fact that the covenant doctrine
of the creeds, whatever it may be, does not produce a teaching
of justification by faith and works, nor a teaching of an election
unto grace that nevertheless fails to save, nor a teaching that
covenant saints can fall away from Christ and perish.

The very name of the theology and movement demands
that any criticism of the federal vision treat its doctrine of the
covenant. That the Reformed critics of the federal vision fail
to do so is inexcusable. Were I to assign a seminary student to

critique the federal vision, and the result was a paper that examined all aspects of the federal vision except the fundamental teaching expressed by its name, I would mark the paper with an "F"—not for federal, but for failure.

That the federal vision is a doctrine of the covenant is also evident from the fact that the men of the federal vision defend their various teachings, when they come under attack, by appeal to their doctrine of the covenant. This was their defense at the well-known Knox Theological Seminary Colloquium in 2003. Leading proponents and some carefully selected, mild critics of the federal vision gathered to discuss the theology of the federal vision. The papers of both the proponents and the critics concentrated on the federal vision's doctrine of the covenant. Justification, perseverance, baptism, election, and other doctrines necessarily came up in the discussion, but the main subject was the covenant.[1]

More precisely, the main subject was the covenant of God *with the children of believing parents.* Opening the colloquium, Douglas Wilson forthrightly confronted the assembled theologians with the fundamental issue at the meeting and with a "fundamental concern" of the federal vision.

> One of the fundamental concerns is this: we want to insist upon believing God's promises concerning our children. This is just another way of believing that God will preserve His covenant people over time. We affirm the perseverance of the *saints,* and not just the perseverance of one individual saint. But the saints extend over generations. The promises do not come to detached individuals. Covenant children are placed in covenant homes by a sovereign God, and we are required as Christians to believe the promises of Scripture concerning these children.[2]

1   The papers have been published as the book *The Auburn Avenue Theology, Pros & Cons: Debating the Federal Vision.*

2   Douglas Wilson, "Union with Christ: An Overview of the Federal Vision," in ibid., 2–3.

Summing up the conference in the last chapter, the moderator, indicating what the federal vision is all about, applauded the federal vision for its "renewed emphasis on the importance of the covenant."[3] Further evidence that the federal vision is fundamentally a doctrine of the covenant is that the men of the federal vision promote their theology by explaining and arguing their distinctive doctrine of the covenant. Shepherd's seminal book, *The Call of Grace*, is subtitled *How the Covenant Illuminates Salvation and Evangelism*. Attempting to ground the covenant doctrine of the federal vision in the reformers, Peter Lillback has written a book titled *The Binding of God: Calvin's Role in the Development of Covenant Theology*.[4]

Indeed, the *critics* of the federal vision perceive the federal vision as a certain, definite doctrine of the covenant. They never act on the perception, but they recognize what is, after all, unmistakable. Guy Waters, who is touted as one of the most reliable critics of the federal vision, titled his critique of the federal vision *The Federal Vision and Covenant Theology*.[5] Waters did not, in fact, do what the title of his book promises, namely, expose and refute the covenant doctrine that is the root of the federal vision—not at all!—but he did at least acknowledge the root of the federal vision.

In 1982, after seven years of continual controversy over his teachings, especially his denial of justification by faith alone, the board of Westminster Seminary finally "removed" Professor Norman Shepherd. Their explanation to the public stated that "the problems in his teaching [especially his teaching of justification by faith and by works]...*are inherent in his view of the 'covenant dynamic'....It is in the distinctive elements*

3 E. Calvin Beisner, "Concluding Comments on the Federal Vision," in ibid., 305. Commending the federal vision for renewing emphasis on the covenant is akin to praising al-Qaeda for renewing emphasis on bomb making.

4 Peter A. Lillback, *The Binding of God: Calvin's Role in the Development of Covenant Theology* (Grand Rapids, MI: Baker, 2001).

5 Guy Prentiss Waters, *The Federal Vision and Covenant Theology: A Comparative Analysis* (Phillipsburg, NJ: P&R, 2006).

and emphases of his theology of the covenant that the problem [especially his doctrine of justification by works] *appears.*"[6] Of particular concern in Shepherd's teaching, the board went on to say, was "the omission of any clear treatment of Christ as the covenant Head."[7] Rejection of Christ's headship of the covenant of grace is basic to, and a hallmark of, the covenant doctrine that Shepherd and the other men of the federal vision embrace and develop.

Because the federal vision is a theology of the covenant, no criticism of the federal vision is effective that does not address the federal vision's doctrine of the covenant. No criticism that fails to address the federal vision's covenant doctrine can be taken seriously. All such criticism is superficial, even irrelevant, indeed dangerous. The malignant tumor remains securely in the body of Reformed and Presbyterian churches.

THE DISTINCTIVE COVENANT DOCTRINE
OF THE FEDERAL VISION

What is the distinctive covenant doctrine of the federal vision? What is its supposedly new vision regarding the covenant of God in Jesus Christ? What is this covenant doctrine that manifests itself in the teaching of justification by works? in the teaching of an election of many unto grace and salvation in time that nevertheless fails to assure their eternal salvation? in the teaching of a saving grace that can be resisted and lost? in the teaching of the falling away of many into hell who once truly believed and enjoyed union with Christ?

It is the distinctive teaching of the federal vision's fundamental doctrine of the covenant that the covenant is conditional. The covenant of God depends upon us humans with whom God establishes his covenant. Because the federal vision is especially a doctrine of the covenant with regard to the baptized babies of

---

6   "Reasons and Specifications Supporting the Action of the Board of Trustees in Removing Professor Shepherd, Approved by the Executive Committee of the Board, February 26, 1982," in Robbins, *Companion to the Current Justification Controversy*, 148; emphasis added.

7   Ibid., 154.

believers, the distinctive covenant doctrine of the federal vision holds that the covenant depends upon baptized infants.

There cannot be any doubt about this description of the covenant doctrine of the federal vision. No one can successfully challenge this analysis. The men of the federal vision themselves tell us that this is their covenant doctrine.

For seven years Norman Shepherd informed his interrogators at Westminster Seminary and his judges at the presbytery of the Orthodox Presbyterian Church that his teaching of justification by works is an aspect of his doctrine of a conditional covenant. At one point in the proceedings, therefore, a critic of Shepherd's teaching on justification called attention to the fact that Shepherd's doctrine of justification is embedded "in the context of his distinctive 'covenantal perspective.'" The attempt to have the faculty and board of Westminster Seminary consider Shepherd's "'covenant concept' in relation to justification" was shot down.[8]

When O. Palmer Robertson, a participant in the Shepherd controversy at Westminster Seminary, "summarize[s] the distinctiveness of Shepherd's formulations that generated this controversy," his first observation concerning the source and cause of the controversy is Shepherd's distinctive doctrine of the covenant. In defense of his teachings, particularly justification by works, Shepherd insisted that "justification be understood in terms of the dynamic of the covenant model."[9]

Shepherd's "covenant model" is a conditional covenant.

Shepherd tells the world in *The Call of Grace* that the root of all his teachings is the doctrine of a conditional covenant. In the book Shepherd denies that the covenant with Abraham—the covenant that becomes the new covenant in Jesus Christ—is unconditional. Rather, "conditions were, indeed, attached to the fulfillment of the promises made to Abraham."[10] With explicit reference to the new covenant in Christ, Shepherd

8   Robertson, *The Current Justification Controversy*, 54–55.

9   Ibid., 90.

10 Shepherd, *Call of Grace*, 14.

writes, "Grace is not without condition."[11] Shepherd is saying that the fundamental explanation of all his teachings, particularly justification by good works, is the doctrine of a conditional covenant. Justification by works is fruit; the root is a conditional covenant.

In the book that the men of the federal vision wrote to explain and defend their teachings, John Barach, then a minister in the United Reformed Churches, was given the honor of authoring the first chapter of exposition. The reason is that his topic lays the foundation for all the doctrines that follow, including justification. Barach's topic is the covenant. Indicating that the men of the federal vision are well aware of the basic issue in the current controversy over the covenant (which all the non-Protestant Reformed critics of the federal vision pretend not to notice and are determined not to see—the proverbial four-hundred-pound gorilla in the kitchen), the precise topic of Barach's foundational contribution is "Covenant and Election."

Barach is clear and forthright concerning the distinctive covenant doctrine of the federal vision: "God truly brings those people into His covenant, into union with Christ...[causes them] to share in His blessings [and] experience His love." Nevertheless, they eventually fall away and perish eternally in hell. The reason, declares Barach, is that "the covenant relationship is conditional."[12]

ORIGINS OF THE CONDITIONAL COVENANT

This doctrine of a conditional covenant, which is the root of all the teachings of the federal vision, is not new with the men of the federal vision, as the word "vision" in their name for their theology might suggest. This covenant doctrine did not spring full-blown from the head of Norman Shepherd, as Athena from the head of Zeus. It is not a doctrine of the covenant that Reformed theologians had never heard of before Shepherd, Gaffin, Barach, Schlissel, and Wilson came on the scene.

11 Ibid., 63.

12 John Barach, "Covenant and Election," in *The Federal Vision*, ed. Steve Wilkins and Duane Garner (Monroe, LA: Athanasius Press, 2004), 7.

What is new about the federal vision, what is visionary about it, is its *bold development* of an old doctrine of the covenant.

The conditional covenant doctrine of the federal vision is the doctrine of the covenant of the Dutch Reformed theologians Klaas Schilder, Benne Holwerda, and Cornelis Veenhof; of the Reformed Churches in the Netherlands (liberated); of the Canadian Reformed Churches and the American Reformed Churches in North America; and of the Free Reformed Churches in Australia.

The men of the federal vision *advertise* their theology as the covenant doctrine of Schilder and the liberated churches. The federal vision *claims* to be the development of the liberated doctrine of the covenant—such a development as teaches justification by works; as teaches the divine election, *in the sense of Ephesians 1:4*, of every baptized child, Esau as well as Jacob, implying that election can fail to save or, as Douglas Wilson expresses it, "devolve[s] into reprobation";[13] as teaches an ineffectual death of Christ for all the baptized babies of believers; and as teaches the possibility of the falling away of saved covenant saints.

The critics of the federal vision know that the federal vision is developing Schilder's and the liberated churches' covenant doctrine. At the Knox Colloquium, Carl Robbins, one of the critics, said to the house:

> I've finally grasped that he [John Barach, as a spokesman of the federal vision] is simply re-stating the distinctive [covenant theology] of the "Liberated" Reformed Churches. Therefore, it must fairly be pointed out that Pastor Barach cannot be charged with "theological novelty," for his views were first propounded by Klaas Schilder in the 1940s and (before him) Calvin Seminary

---

13   Douglas Wilson, *"Reformed" Is Not Enough: Recovering the Objectivity of the Covenant* (Moscow, ID: Canon Press, 2002), 140–41. Wilson is quoting another writer with approval: "We should not drive a wedge between 'special' and 'covenantal' elections, for special election simply is covenantal election for those who, by God's sovereign electing grace, persevere. For those who fall away, covenantal election devolves into reprobation."

Professor William W. Heyns from the early 1900s. In fact, Pastor Barach has simply and faithfully re-stated those covenantal understandings.[14]

In fact, the doctrine of a conditional covenant, now being developed by the federal vision, goes back a long way further than Klaas Schilder and William Heyns. It is the covenant doctrine of two nineteenth-century Dutch Reformed ministers, K. J. Pieters and J. R. Kreulen, who grievously troubled the Reformed churches of the Secession in the Netherlands.[15] The doctrine of the covenant of Pieters and Kreulen was that of Jacob Arminius in the late sixteenth century, as subtly adjusted by Moyse Amyraut in the early seventeenth century.[16]

It is a doctrine of the covenant that teaches that God is gracious to all the baptized infants of believers without exception. In his grace he establishes the covenant of grace with all without exception. However, whether a particular infant is saved in the covenant, by this covenant grace, depends upon the infant's performing conditions.

14   Carl D. Robbins, "A Response to 'Covenant and Election,'" in *Auburn Avenue Theology*, 157.

15   For a description of the covenant doctrine of K. J. Pieters and J. R. Kreulen and an account of the controversy it caused in the churches of the Secession (*Afscheiding*), see David J. Engelsma, "The Covenant Doctrine of the Fathers of the Secession," in *Always Reforming: Continuation of the Sixteenth-Century Reformation*, ed. David J. Engelsma (Jenison, MI: Reformed Free Publishing Association, 2009), 100–136. See also David J. Engelsma, *Covenant and Election in the Reformed Tradition* (Jenison, MI: Reformed Free Publishing Association, 2011), 9–14.

16   For the covenant doctrine of Jacob Arminius, of which the hallmark was conditionality and of which the doctrine of Moyse Amyraut was only a clever variation, see William den Boer, *God's Twofold Love: The Theology of Jacob Arminius (1559–1609)*, trans. Albert Gootjes (Gottingen: Vandenhoeck & Ruprecht, 2010). Th. Marius van Leeuwen correctly describes Amyrauldism as "a covenant theology" of "two covenant parties: God with his universal offer of salvation...and Man, who gives or gives not his response to that offer" (*Arminius, Arminianism, and Europe: Jacobus Arminius [1559/60–1609]*, ed. Th. Marius van Leeuwen, Keith D. Stangelin, and Marijke Tolsma, Brill's Series in Church History, vol. 39 [Leiden/Boston: Brill, 2009], xix). In Amyrauldism God's covenant offer is conditioned by man's covenant response. Substitute "promise" for "offer" and you have the doctrine of the covenant of Pieters and Kreulen, of Schilder and the liberated, and of the federal vision.

The doctrine of the covenant now being developed by the federal vision holds that the grace of the covenant, particularly with regard to the baptized infants of believers, does not have its source in, nor is determined by, the eternal decree of election. Grace in the covenant is wider than the eternal decree (if, in the thinking of those who hold this covenant doctrine, there is an eternal decree at all).

The covenant doctrine of the federal vision, therefore, is essentially that condemned by the Synod of Dordt. Against the Arminian doctrine that the death of Christ merely allowed God to make his covenant with all humans alike, *conditionally* (the condition being their faith), the Canons of Dordt affirm that, in accordance with the eternal decree of predestination, the death of Christ "confirmed" the covenant with the elect. In addition, striking deliberately—and fatally—at the Arminian notion that faith is a condition unto the continuation of the covenant and unto final covenant salvation, the Canons affirm that the death of Christ purchased faith for the elect and that Christ confers faith upon the elect. Faith is a covenant gift, not a covenant condition.

> It was the [eternal, unconditional] will of God, that Christ by the blood of the cross, *whereby he confirmed the new covenant*, should effectually redeem out of every people, tribe, nation, and language, all those, and those only, who were from eternity chosen to salvation...[and] that he should *confer upon them faith, which...he purchased for them by his death.*[17]

The Canons reject the teaching that God makes the new covenant conditionally with elect and nonelect humans alike, whether adults or baptized infants.

> Synod *rejects* the errors of those...who teach that it was...the purpose of the death of Christ...only that He should acquire for the Father the mere right to establish with man such a covenant as He might please, whether of grace or works...[and]

---

17 Canons of Dordt, 2.8, in *Creeds of Christendom*, 3:587; emphasis added.

> who teach that Christ...merited for the Father only the
> authority or the perfect will to deal again with man, and
> to prescribe new conditions as He might desire...[and]
>
> who teach that the new covenant of grace...does not
> herein consist that we by faith, inasmuch as it accepts
> the merits of Christ, are justified before God and saved,
> but in the fact that God, having revoked the demand of
> perfect obedience of the law, regards faith itself and the
> obedience of faith, although imperfect, as the perfect
> obedience of the law, and does esteem it worthy of the
> reward of eternal life through grace.[18]

Regardless of the further, ignoble ancestry of the covenant doctrine of the federal vision, both the men of the federal vision and their critics agree that the conditional covenant doctrine of the federal vision is that of the liberated Reformed churches.

The Canadian Reformed Churches are disingenuous, therefore, when they profess that the federal vision is not an issue in their churches. Of course it is not an issue. It is their doctrine of the covenant that the federal vision is developing and spreading far and wide.

The conditional covenant doctrine of the federal vision is the doctrine of the covenant that the Protestant Reformed Churches rejected and condemned in the early 1950s, when this doctrine gained entrance into the churches by the direct, personal efforts of Klaas Schilder. The Protestant Reformed Churches condemned the liberated doctrine of a conditional covenant as Arminianism in the covenant. This the federal vision is proving it to be, beyond any shadow of doubt.

Inasmuch as the federal vision is the development of the covenant doctrine of the liberated Reformed, the Declaration of Principles of the Protestant Reformed Churches, concerning the covenant, ought to be the most sought after and highly prized document in the community of Reformed and Presbyterian

---

18   Canons of Dordt, 2, Rejection of Errors 2–4, in *Confessions and Church Order*, 164–65. Schaff does not include the rejection of errors sections of the Canons in English.

churches in North America. This is the document by which the Protestant Reformed Churches exposed and condemned the liberated doctrine of a conditional covenant. It is *the* manual for detecting and eradicating the root of the heresy in the Reformed churches that is the federal vision.[19]

19   The Declaration of Principles is found in *Confessions and Church Order*, 409–31.

THE ROOT OF THE FEDERAL VISION   3

Conditions | Ignoring the Root

The doctrine of a conditional covenant now being developed by the federal vision is the teaching that God on his part is gracious to all the baptized babies of believing members of the church alike. Whether this grace abides with a child and is effective to bring a child to everlasting salvation in Abraham's bosom, however, depend upon conditions that the child must perform. The conditions are the child's faith and obedience. Some children perform the conditions and are saved. Others— *many* others—fail to perform the conditions and go lost, despite the fact that God was as gracious to them as he was to those who are saved.

According to the federal vision, God has a gracious attitude toward every child of godly parents. He desires to save every child. At the baptism of the children of believers, God actually bestows the grace of the covenant upon every baptized child alike. Here, the federal vision becomes guilty of a form of the false doctrine of baptismal regeneration. Call it the federal vision doctrine of baptismal covenant salvation.

This covenant grace, of which every child is a recipient, is *saving* grace, the grace of God in the crucified and risen Christ. That it is saving grace does not mean that it irresistibly saves every child or, for that matter, any child. It does not. But the meaning is that this grace would save, would bring the child to heaven, *if* the child performs the conditions.

The meaning is also that this covenant grace saves *temporarily*. It unites every baptized child to Christ in the bond of the covenant, so that every child begins to receive the life of Christ. The federal vision appeals to John 15:1–17, Jesus' teaching of the branches and the vine, in support of its contention that every child alike is spiritually, truly, and savingly united to Christ. This grace brings to every baptized child, without exception, the blessings of the new covenant, including justification.

Basic to the federal vision's doctrine is that the covenant promise, which is the gracious oath of God, "I will be your God, and you will be my child," comes to every child alike at his or her baptism. By the coming of the promise to every child alike, the federal vision does not mean only that every child, upon coming to years of understanding, hears the promise that God will save the child who believes. Not at all! Rather, the federal vision means that God addresses the promise to every infant alike. God makes the promise to every infant personally, as the expression of God's grace toward that child and of God's desire for that child's salvation.

By the covenant promise to every child at baptism, God actually establishes his covenant with every baptized child. He unites every child to Christ.

At this point it is important to the federal vision, as to the covenant doctrine of the liberated Reformed that the federal vision is developing, to deny that Christ is the head of the covenant of grace. If Christ is head of the covenant, God makes the covenant with Jesus Christ *and with those who are Christ's by divine election*, and with no one else. If Christ is head of the covenant—the legal representative of all who are in the covenant of grace—God makes the covenant promise to Christ *and to those who are Christ's by divine election*, and to no one else. There was a reason, as the board of Westminster Seminary observed, that Professor Norman Shepherd's doctrine of the covenant omitted the covenant headship of Christ. The whole of his doctrine of a conditional covenant depended on omitting the headship of Christ.[1]

This "omission," which signaled a denial, of the headship of Christ brought Shepherd into direct and open conflict with the Westminster Larger Catechism: "With whom was the covenant of grace made? The covenant of grace was made with Christ as the second Adam, and in him with all the elect as his seed."[2]

CONDITIONS

The covenant with its grace, however, according to the federal vision, is conditional. From beginning to end, it is conditional. Covenant grace depends for its saving efficacy upon works that the child must do. The men of the federal vision sum up these works as lifelong covenant faithfulness.

The gracious attitude of God toward all the baptized babies alike is conditional.

The covenant union with Christ established at or by baptism is conditional.

The babies' possession and enjoyment of all the covenant blessings, including justification, are conditional.

Everlasting covenant salvation in the new world in the day of Christ is conditional.

By covenant condition the federal vision does not mean what the reformers meant and what the Westminster standards mean with the occasional use of "condition" in their doctrine of the covenant. By condition the reformers and the Westminster standards have strictly in mind the necessary means by which God fulfills his covenant promise to the elect and thus realizes his covenant with them.

---

1 "Reasons and Specifications Supporting the Action of the Board of Trustees in Removing Professor Shepherd, Approved by the Executive Committee of the Board, February 26, 1982," in Robbins, *Companion to the Current Justification Controversy*, 148.

2 Westminster Larger Catechism, Q&A 31, in *Confession of Faith and Subordinate Standards, The Free Church of Scotland* (Edinburgh: repr. William Blackwood & Sons, 1973), 57.

The federal vision means something radically different. Covenant condition for the federal vision refers to works of the child upon which the covenant, its promise, its grace, and its salvation depend. Covenant condition for the federal vision is a work of the child by which the child distinguishes himself from other children who are objects of the same gracious promise and recipients of the same grace. Covenant condition for the federal vision is a work of the child that makes covenant grace effectual in his salvation, whereas without the work covenant grace would be impotent. Covenant condition for the federal vision is a work of the child without which covenant grace is resisted, frustrated, and lost.

That this is what the federal vision means by condition is evident from its teachings that a child can resist God's covenant grace, which was once given to him personally, and go everlastingly lost; that a child can frustrate the gracious covenant promise, which God made to him personally, and go lost; that a child can separate himself from Christ, to whom he was really united, and go lost; that a child can forfeit and lose all the blessings of salvation, which he once possessed and enjoyed, and go lost; and that a child can fall away from the love of God in Christ, which once God had for him, and perish eternally in the hatred of God.

According to the federal vision, many do fall away, lose grace, and perish because they do not perform the conditions. The federal vision is not embarrassed by this doctrine, but seemingly glories in it. The men of the federal vision emphasize it as one of their most important teachings. They call Reformed churches and parents to warn their children of this sword of Damocles hanging over their heads until the moment of their death, as though this dreadful threat will scare the children into living godly lives, that is, nervously performing the conditions of the covenant.

This doctrine of a conditional covenant is the root of the federal vision. Justification by faith and works is the bitter fruit. According to Galatians 3:8, the main blessing of God's covenant with Abraham is that "God would justify the heathen through faith." If the covenant itself is conditional, that is, dependent on our works, so also is justification conditional, that is, dependent on our works.

But if justification is conditional, so also is every aspect of salvation conditional, for justification is the heart of the gospel. The fruit of the federal vision doctrine of a conditional covenant is the denial of all the doctrines of sovereign grace—the denial of sovereign grace *in the covenant*.

In the covenant, election is God's choice of all the infants, *conditionally*.

In the covenant, the atonement of the cross was for all the infants, *conditionally*.

In the covenant, grace—*saving* grace—is for, and even in, all the infants alike, *conditionally*.

In the covenant, all can fall away from Christ and salvation and perish, because God's preservation is *conditional*.

The bitter fruit of the federal vision's doctrine of a conditional covenant is an election that fails to save; a cross that fails to redeem; a grace that is resistible; and the falling away of saints—*in the covenant*.

Steve Wilkins, a prominent spokesman of the federal vision, announced the theology of the federal vision, root and fruit, to the Knox Colloquium.

> Covenant, therefore, is a gracious relationship [between God and every baptized child]...To be in covenant is to have the treasures of God's mercy and grace and the love which He has for His own Son given to you [that is, to every baptized child, including those who perish]. But the covenant is not *unconditional*. It requires persevering faithfulness.[3]

Because the covenant is conditional, Wilkins added, it is very well possible that one who was graciously united to Christ, possessed all the treasures of God's mercy and grace, and was

3 Steve Wilkins, "Covenant, Baptism, and Salvation," in *Auburn Avenue Theology*, 265–66; the emphasis is Wilkins'.

the object of God's love "forfeits all that was his by virtue of his union with Christ in covenant."[4]

IGNORING THE ROOT

About the root of the federal vision—its distinctive doctrine of the covenant—a root that produces the fruit of the denial of the gospel of salvation by grace alone in its entirety, there is now, and has been for the past ten years and more (since the publication of Shepherd's *The Call of Grace*), *silence*—earnest, studied, deliberate, deafening, astounding, inexcusable, blameworthy *silence*.

Some theologians and churches have condemned the federal vision's denial of justification by faith alone. Some have gone on record as affirming the five points of Calvinism. But not one has addressed the federal vision's doctrine of the covenant. Not one has been radical, that is, has gotten to the root of the federal vision. Not one has cut to the cancerous tumor in the Reformed body.

The adoption by the 2010 synod of the United Reformed Churches of a report of a committee that had been mandated to study the federal vision is a perfect instance of the refusal of the Reformed churches to critique the federal vision at its root.

The report consists of fifteen affirmations of salvation by grace, concentrating on justification by faith alone. The fifteen affirmations are sound. The decision adopting them is weak: "Synod urge[s] all office-bearers to repudiate Federal Vision teachings where they are not in harmony with the following articles from the three forms of unity."[5] The synod merely "urged" officebearers to repudiate unspecified errors of the federal vision. It was only the officebearers who were thus urged.

Worst of all regarding the decision, synod urged the officebearers to repudiate federal vision teachings "where they are

4   Ibid., 269.

5   This decision and the "15 Affirmations" are given in the report on Synod London 2010 of the United Reformed Churches by Glenda Mathes in "Federal Vision and Justification: Unequivocal unanimity," *Christian Renewal* (August 18, 2010): 8–10.

not in harmony" with the creeds. This left up to each office-bearer to decide for himself where the federal vision is not in accord with the creeds. Indeed, it left up to each officebearer to decide for himself *whether* the federal vision is out of accord with the creeds. It is possible that some officebearers in the United Reformed Churches decide that the federal vision is not out of accord with the creeds at all, but is perfectly orthodox. This is exactly the contention of the men of the federal vision in the various Reformed and Presbyterian churches. James Jordan, a vocal advocate of federal vision theology, has already responded to the decision of the United Reformed Churches on the federal vision by declaring that the federal vision is per-fectly orthodox regarding every one of the fifteen affirmations of the United Reformed Churches with the possible exception of paedocommunion (child communion), which is of no great importance to the United Reformed Churches in any case.[6]

Suppose that Dordt had made something like the United Reformed Churches' decision: Synod urges the officebearers to repudiate Arminian teachings where they are not in harmony with the Bible, the Heidelberg Catechism, and the Belgic Confession. We would all be five-point Arminians today. Dordt specified the false doctrines of Arminianism, condemned them, and required every officebearer and every member of the Reformed churches to join in the condemnation.

What the United Reformed synod ought to have decided is this: With regard to its doctrine of justification by faith and works and with regard to its denial of all the doctrines of salvation by sovereign grace in the covenant, synod declares the federal vision a heresy and advises every consistory vigorously to expose and condemn the federal vision, so that every member of the United Reformed Churches, man, woman, and child, is protected against this God-dishonoring and soul-destroying bringing up again of Arminianism out of hell.[7]

6   See Jordan's letter to the editor in *Christian Renewal* (September 15, 2010).

7   Canons of Dordt, 2, Rejection of Errors 3 charges against Arminian theologians that by their doctrine they "bring again out of hell the Pelagian

And then the synod of the United Reformed Churches ought to have added: fruit *and root*, that is, synod declares the federal vision heretical in its root, as well as in its fruit.

The glaring fault of the decision of the United Reformed Churches is that it does not expose and cut out the root of the federal vision: its doctrine of the covenant.

There is not one word about the covenant doctrine of the federal vision, whence the bitter fruit of justification by works grows. Not one of the fifteen affirmations affirms the following: Against the theology of the federal vision, synod declares that the covenant of God with his people in Jesus Christ is a covenant of grace, not of works; being saved in this covenant is "dependent on the special gift of mercy, which powerfully works in [one],"[8] not on one's appropriating salvation by his own efforts; and the covenant is sure and steadfast with every elect believer and every elect child of believers, in whom the grace of the covenant is begun, because God is faithful who has promised.

Because the decision fails to get at the root of the federal vision, the decision of the United Reformed Churches is of little worth. Indeed, it is positively dangerous. It assures the believers and their children in the United Reformed Churches that the threat is gone, when, in fact, the cancerous tumor remains. The doctor has merely removed one of the cancerous lumps on the surface of the body.

error" (*Confessions and Church Order*, 165).

8   See Canons of Dordt, 2, Rejection of Errors 6, in ibid., 164, 166: "Synod *rejects* the errors of those...who use the difference between meriting and appropriating, to the end that they may instill into the minds of the imprudent and inexperienced this teaching, that God, as far as He is concerned, has been minded of applying to all equally the benefits gained by the death of Christ; but that, while some obtain the pardon of sin and eternal life and others do not, this difference depends on their own free will, which joins itself to the grace that is offered without exception, and that it is not dependent on the special gift of mercy, which powerfully works in them, that they rather than others should appropriate unto themselves this grace." Identify those to whom God "has been minded of applying...equally the benefits gained by the death of Christ" and to whom "grace...is offered without exception" as the baptized children of believers, and it is immediately evident that this condemnation falls on the covenant doctrine of the federal vision.

Just this false assurance was given to the members of the United Reformed Churches by the reporter of the synodical decision: "Synod 2010 proved that the federation is united in its commitment to refuting the errors of the Federal Vision."[9] "All is well!"

"The church body has been healed and is now healthy!"

But what if the root of the federal vision remains, deep in the body, full of death and malignant vigor—the malignant vigor that has already produced *in the United Reformed Churches* the bold denial of justification by faith alone and an open repudiation of all the doctrines of grace?

Well then, the synod of the United Reformed Churches healed the hurt of God's people "slightly," saying, "Peace and health," when there is no peace and health (Jer. 6:14).

Spokesmen of the United Reformed Churches defend the synodical decision by pointing out that a previous synod had mandated the study committee to restrict itself to the federal vision doctrine of justification, that is, to restrict itself to an analysis of the heretical fruit, while ignoring the root of the heresy. This defense does not exonerate the recent synod, or the study committee, but rather implicates the previous synod.

What team of physicians orders its surgeons to restrict themselves to the cancerous lump on the surface of the body, while deliberately ignoring the malignant tumor that lies deeper in the body? And what conscientious surgeons will heed this incredible instruction as they operate? And what team of physicians will congratulate themselves, and the cancerous patient, after the surgeons, caring for their instruction but not for the patient, have removed the lump but left the tumor?

9 Mathes, "Federal Vision and Justification," *Christian Renewal* (August 18, 2010), 8.

TAKING HOLD OF THE ROOT   4

Ignoring Side Issues | False Doctrine
Uprooting the Heresy | The Unconditional Covenant
The Slander of Antinomianism

The fundamental doctrine of the federal vision—its teaching of a conditional covenant—must be taken hold of and refuted.

IGNORING SIDE ISSUES

I note in passing that although the critics of the federal vision leave this fundamental doctrine of the federal vision strictly alone, they do make themselves busy with two comparatively incidental aspects of the truth of the covenant that come up in connection with the theology of the federal vision: the covenant with Adam in paradise before the fall and the covenant with Israel.

Regarding both of these incidental aspects of the biblical truth of the covenant—incidental in the controversy over the federal vision—the critics distinguish themselves by going seriously wrong. Addressing the covenant with Adam, the would-be critics of the federal vision insist that the covenant with Adam was a covenant of works *in the sense that Adam could have merited with God by not eating the forbidden fruit and that what he could have merited was nothing less than the eternal, immortal, heavenly life that Christ earned for the elect church by his death and created by his resurrection.*

According to these would-be critics, Adam could have accomplished for all humans that which Christ accomplished only for some. Adam could have put God in his debt, so that eternal life for the human race might have been God's payment of what Adam—a mere man—earned. To all eternity, the human race might have sung, loudly, "This heaven with its eternal life is what we merited! Glory be to us!"[1]

With regard to the covenant with Israel, some prominent critics of the federal vision are teaching that the covenant with Israel was a restoration of the covenant of works with Adam, at least in part. Thus meritorious works are introduced into the old covenant—the covenant that the Reformed faith has always explained as *essentially the same as the new covenant in Christ*.[2]

But these two aspects of the truth of the covenant and their treatment by critics of the federal vision may be ignored. They are beside the point in the controversy with the federal vision.

The issue in the controversy with the federal vision is the conditional covenant.

The federal vision is not fundamentally a doctrine of the covenant with Adam. Nor is it fundamentally a doctrine of the Sinaitic covenant.

Fundamentally, it is a doctrine of the new covenant with the church in Jesus Christ, the fulfillment of the covenant with Abraham. Fundamentally, it is a doctrine of the covenant with baptized children of the New Testament church.

Read Shepherd's *The Call of Grace*.

Read the explanation and defense of their theology by the men of the federal vision themselves in *The Auburn Avenue Theology* and in *The Federal Vision*.

---

1   For thorough treatments of the covenant with Adam, affirming a creation covenant but denying a meritorious contract, see David J. Engelsma, "The Covenant of Creation with Adam," *Protestant Reformed Theological Journal* 40, no. 1 (November 2006): 3–42; and Nathan J. Langerak, "A Critique of the Covenant of Works in Contemporary Controversy," *Protestant Reformed Theological Journal* 44, no. 2 (April 2011): 3–53.

2   On the relation of the old covenant and the new covenant, see John Calvin, *Institutes of the Christian Religion*, ed. John T. McNeill, trans. Ford Lewis Battles (Philadelphia: Westminster Press, 1960), 2.7–11, 1:348–464. For an exegetical and doctrinal demonstration that the old covenant of Sinai was wholly a covenant of grace, not at all a covenant of meritorious works, and that there can be and may be no restoration of the covenant with Adam, see Engelsma, *Covenant and Election*, 209–19.

The bitter fruit of the federal vision indicates the root. The federal vision doctrine of justification by faith and works is not some fruit of an erroneous view of the covenant with Adam, or of a mistaken doctrine of the covenant at Sinai. It is the fruit of a certain doctrine of the new covenant in Christ. And as we have seen, this is the doctrine of a covenant of conditional grace and conditional salvation.

FALSE DOCTRINE

The federal vision's doctrine of a conditional covenant with all the baptized children of believers alike—the root of the federal vision—is false doctrine, according to Scripture and the Reformed confessions.

It is false doctrine, first, in that it teaches that salvation, in the covenant, depends upon the sinner, upon the sinful, baptized infant, upon what that sinful infant will do, namely, perform the conditions of believing and obeying. Scripture denies this: "[Salvation] is not of him that willeth, nor of him that runneth, but of God that sheweth mercy" (Rom. 9:16). The text that immediately precedes in Romans 9 teaches that the mercy of God, upon which the salvation of circumcised babies once depended and upon which the salvation of baptized babies now depends, is sovereign, discriminating mercy: "For he saith to Moses, I will have mercy on whom I will have mercy" (v. 15).

Why should the doctrine that salvation depends only upon the sovereign mercy of God be true on the mission field, but not in the covenant?

The fact is, Romans 9:16 refers to salvation *in the covenant.* The apostle is drawing a conclusion from God's word to Moses in Exodus 33:19 concerning God's salvation of some in distinction from others among the circumcised offspring of Abraham. In the sphere of the covenant, with regard to infants who had the sign of the covenant in their flesh, God said, "I will be gracious to whom I will be gracious and will shew mercy on whom I will shew mercy" (Ex. 33:19).

The federal vision's doctrine of a conditional covenant is false doctrine, second, in that it teaches that, in the covenant, one child makes himself to differ from other children with regard to salvation. According to the federal vision, all alike are united to Christ and all alike receive the grace of God. That one is everlastingly saved in distinction from others who are not saved is because the one performed the conditions of the covenant, whereas the others did not.

This teaching is contrary to the gospel of the apostle, who asks, rhetorically, "Who maketh thee to differ from another? and what hast thou [baptized child of believers, including faith and obedience] that thou didst not receive?" (1 Cor. 4:7).

The federal vision's doctrine of a conditional covenant is false doctrine, third, in that it teaches grace—*saving* grace—in the covenant that can be and often is resisted. Here, the federal vision nails its Arminian colors to the mast! The very heart and core and essence of the Arminian heresy condemned by Dordt was, and is, the doctrine of a grace of God, wider in extent than election unto salvation, that can be resisted by sinners. The implication of the doctrine of resistible grace is that those who are saved by this resistible grace are saved, not by the grace, but by their will, which makes the grace effectual.

The men of the federal vision are clear about their teaching of resistible grace in the covenant. The "Summary Statement of [Auburn Avenue Presbyterian Church]...on the Covenant, Baptism, and Salvation"—a quasi-official federal vision statement of belief—confesses that all baptized children receive "the same initial covenant grace," those who perish as well as those who are finally saved.[3] This "initial covenant grace," received by all the baptized children alike, brings all the children "into union with Christ" and causes all to "share in His [Christ's] blessings."[4] It bestows upon all the children "the blessings of the covenant, including the forgiveness of sins, adoption,

---

3 Summary Statement of [Auburn Avenue Presbyterian Church's] Position on the Covenant, Baptism, and Salvation, cited in R. Fowler White, "Covenant and Apostasy," in *Auburn Avenue Theology*, 214.

4 Barach, "Covenant and Election," in *Federal Vision*, 37.

possession of the kingdom, sanctification, etc., and yet [some] apostatize and fall short of the grace of God."[5]

The doctrine of resistible grace is condemned in the third and fourth heads of the Canons of Dordt.

> The Synod *rejects* the errors of those…who teach that God in the regeneration of man does not use such powers of His omnipotence as potently and infallibly bend man's will to faith and conversion; but that all the works of grace having been accomplished, which God employs to convert man, man may yet so resist God and the Holy Spirit when God intends man's regeneration and wills to regenerate him, and indeed that man often does so resist, that he prevents entirely his regeneration, and that it therefore remains in man's power to be regenerated or not.[6]

The Reformed faith confesses the sovereignty of grace,

> a supernatural work, most powerful…not inferior in efficacy to creation or the resurrection from the dead… so that all in whose hearts God works in this marvelous manner are certainly, infallibly, and effectually regenerated, and do actually believe.[7]

The federal vision's doctrine of a conditional covenant is false doctrine, fourth, in that it teaches that the gracious covenant promise of God, the awesome oath of God upon which everything depends—covenant, covenant blessings, covenant preservation, and covenant glory—can fail and does fail in many instances. According to the federal vision, when God gave the covenant promise to Abraham and his "seed," in Genesis 17, God made the promise to every physical descendant of Abraham. Today, at baptism, God makes the promise to every baptized child: "I swear by myself that I will be your

5   Wilkins, "Covenant, Baptism, and Salvation," in ibid., 62.

6   Canons of Dordt, 3–4, Rejection of Errors 8, in *Confessions and Church Order*, 170, 172.

7   Canons of Dordt, 3–4.12, in *Creeds of Christendom*, 3:590.

God! I will unite you to Christ! I will save you in this life and in the life to come!"

But the promise fails. It fails because it is conditional and because some children fail to perform the conditions, but it fails.

Douglas Wilson is compelled to acknowledge the failure of the covenant promise in the theology of the federal vision: "Now these promises...have apparent instances of non-fulfillment."[8] "Apparent" is a weasel word. It protects Wilson somewhat from facing the consequences of his blasphemous charge that the promises of God fail. Indicating that he knows full well that he is treading on the holy ground of the great covenant doctrine of Romans 9, Wilson immediately asks, with an eye obviously on Romans 9:6, "Have the promises of God fallen to the ground?"[9]

But the federal vision theologian refuses to answer his, and the apostle's, question as the apostle does in Romans 9:6–29: No! Emphatically, no! "Not as though the word of God [that is, the covenant promise to Abraham in old time and to believing parents today] hath taken none effect" (v. 6).

Why is it not true that the covenant promise has failed, even though multitudes of Abraham's physical, circumcised offspring perished under the old covenant and even though many physical, baptized children of believing parents perish in unbelief today?

Because the promise is conditional, and some children of Abraham failed to perform the conditions?

Absolutely no such thing!

Rather (such is Paul's explanation of the not-failing of the covenant promise), "they are not all Israel, which are of Israel" (v. 6). There are two different kinds of children of Abraham, as there are two different kinds of children of believers today. Some are merely "children of the flesh"; others are "children of the promise" (v. 8). The difference between the two kinds of children is determined by God's predestination, election and

---

8   Wilson, "Union with Christ: An Overview of the Federal Vision," in *Auburn Avenue Theology*, 7.

9   Ibid.

reprobation. Only some, the children of the promise according to election, are counted for the seed of Abraham, and for the seed of believing parents. And the promise—the word of God of verse 6, which has not failed and cannot fail—refers to and is addressed by God to the elect children only. According to Galatians 3:16, the covenant promise that God made to Abraham's "seed" in Genesis 12–24 was a promise to Jesus Christ, as head of the covenant of grace: "Now to Abraham and his seed were the promises made. He saith not, And to seeds, as of many; but as of one, And to thy seed, which is Christ." Verse 29 of Galatians 3 extends the covenant promise (the word of God of Romans 9:6 that has not failed) to those who are "Christ's": "And if ye be Christ's, then are ye Abraham's seed, and heirs according to the promise." Men and women belong to Christ because God gave them to Christ in the decree of election (John 6:37, 39; John 17:2, 6, 9, 11–12, 24).

The federal vision's doctrine of a conditional covenant is false doctrine, fifth, in that it denies that the covenant, the covenant promise, covenant grace, covenant salvation, and, indeed, the head, mediator, and substance of the covenant himself—Jesus the Christ—have their source in, and are determined by, God's election in eternity. Here the scalpel of criticism cuts to the quick of the tumor that is the covenant theology of the federal vision.

The federal vision deliberately cuts the covenant loose from the eternal decree of election. Election, the federal vision contends, does not govern the covenant. Perhaps on the mission field saving grace and salvation are determined by election, but not in the covenant.

To which contention, the question is why? Why should union with Christ, grace, and salvation on the mission field have their source in election, but not grace and salvation in the covenant? Why does not Acts 13:48 apply to the physical children of godly parents? "As many as were ordained to eternal life believed." Yes, and if God's eternal will does not govern the covenant, whose will does govern it?

Romans 9 gives the lie to the federal vision. It is precisely the point of the chapter that grace and salvation *in the covenant*, among the *circumcised sons of Abraham*, more specifically between the *twin sons of believing Isaac and believing Rebekah*, have their source in and are determined by divine, eternal, unconditional election. Before the two sons of Isaac and Rebekah were born or had done good or evil, God loved and chose Jacob unto covenant grace and covenant salvation, and God hated and reprobated Esau.

What was true concerning Jacob and Esau, Romans 9:15 applies to all the physical children of Abraham in the Old Testament. The apostle quotes Exodus 33:19: "I will have mercy on whom I will have mercy." This was the word of God at Sinai, after the sin with the calf, revealing that his sovereign will governs mercy *in the covenant*.

Two additional observations are necessary concerning the denial by the federal vision that election governs the covenant of grace. First, the federal vision errs when it says that the Bible does not make any distinction between two kinds of baptized children and their different relationship to the covenant. Romans 9:6 makes this distinction: Some are merely "of Israel"; others are "Israel." First John 2:19 makes this distinction: Some baptized members of the congregation are merely *among* us, but not truly *of* us. John 10 makes this distinction: Some circumcised Israelites were Jesus' sheep, whereas others were not his sheep and, therefore, did not believe on him.

The Old Testament prophets make this distinction, especially Isaiah: Among the multitude of circumcised Jews was a "remnant." Romans 11:5 calls these comparatively few people "a remnant according to the election of grace," thus attributing the difference of these people from the others—a difference that consisted of faith and salvation—to God's eternal election.

The second observation concerning the federal vision's denial that election governs the covenant is that the federal vision errs when it teaches two kinds of election regarding the covenant: an unconditional election of all the baptized children to receive union with Christ and the justifying grace of God, and a conditional election unto salvation of those children who perform the condition.

The Canons of Dordt condemn this teaching of two kinds of election as the Arminian heresy:

> The Synod *rejects* the errors of those…who teach that there are various kinds of election of God unto eternal life: the one general and indefinite, the other particular and definite; and that the latter in turn is either incomplete, revocable, non-decisive, and conditional, or complete, irrevocable, decisive, and absolute. Likewise: that there is one election unto faith and another unto salvation, so that election can be unto justifying faith without being a decisive election unto salvation…For this is a fancy of men's minds, invented regardless of the Scriptures, whereby the doctrine of election is corrupted, and this golden chain of our salvation is broken: *And whom he foreordained, them he also called; and whom he called, them he also justified; and whom he justified, them he also glorified* (Rom. 8:30).[10]

The federal vision is a "fancy of men's minds, invented regardless of the Scriptures," *concerning the covenant*. It introduces the Arminian heresy *into the doctrine of the covenant of grace.*[11]

---

10 Canons of Dordt, 1, Rejection of Errors 2, in *Confessions and Church Order*, 159–60.

11 As the root of the federal vision is its doctrine of a conditional covenant, the nub of the controversy between the doctrine of the unconditional covenant and the doctrine of a conditional covenant is the relation between covenant and election—election as confessed by the Canons of Dordt, 1.7, the eternal, unconditional decree appointing a certain, definite number unto salvation. For a historical, confessional, doctrinal, and exegetical treatment of this nub of the controversy in light of the federal vision, see Engelsma, *Covenant and Election in the Reformed Tradition.*

UPROOTING THE HERESY

The heretical root of the federal vision—its doctrine of a conditional covenant—must be repudiated. To say it differently, the federal vision's doctrine of conditional, resistible grace in the covenant must be repudiated. If the root is not excised, if churches and theologians content themselves with cutting off fruits and branches (for example, justification by works), the heresy will remain, flourish, and eventually kill the Reformed churches with the dead wood of Arminianism, Roman Catholicism, and Pelagianism.

If the root is allowed to remain in the conservative Reformed and Presbyterian churches, the members may well ask the question whether their seminary professors and ministers are not, in fact, teaching the false doctrine of the federal vision. Probably, they are not yet teaching the heresy of the federal vision in its developed and open form—justification by works—but they are teaching it in its root form: a conditional covenant of resistible grace with all the children alike, governed, not by God's sovereign will of election, but by the children's sovereign will. And the elders are permitting it.

Repudiating the federal vision's doctrine of a conditional covenant, the Reformed churches must embrace and develop the doctrine of the covenant that is perfectly, and obviously, in accord with the gospel of sovereign, particular grace restored by the Reformation and confessed in the Canons of Dordt and in the Westminster Confession of Faith. This doctrine of the covenant is no malignant tumor in the Reformed body, but its natural, healthy growth. It does not question and deny justification by faith alone, but proclaims and defends this fundamental truth of the gospel. This doctrine of the covenant is orthodox. It has an honorable place in the Reformed tradition, running from John Calvin through the Secession theologian Simon van Velzen, and through Herman Bavinck to Herman Hoeksema.[12]

12 For Calvin's doctrine of the covenant, particularly with regard to the children of believers, see his *Institutes*, 4.16, 2:1324–59; and Engelsma, *Covenant and Election in the Reformed Tradition*, 83–161; for the doctrine of the covenant of the fathers of the Secession, including van Velzen, again particularly with

THE UNCONDITIONAL COVENANT

The doctrine of the covenant that is in accord with the Reformation's gospel of sovereign grace is the teaching of the unconditional covenant. This is a covenant of grace, not of conditions. This is a covenant that depends upon the baptizing God, not upon the baptized child.

The doctrine of the unconditional covenant is the doctrine of a covenant governed, as Romans 9 teaches, by the eternal decree of gracious election, accompanied by the equally eternal and sovereign decree of righteous reprobation. "I will have [covenant] mercy on whom I will have [covenant] mercy, and I will have [covenant] compassion on whom I will have [covenant] compassion" (Rom. 9:15, quoting Ex. 33:19).

The doctrine of the unconditional covenant is the doctrine of a covenant established with Christ, as head of the covenant, and with the multitudes of the elect in him, including many, often all, of the children of believing parents. That God has established the covenant with Jesus Christ personally as head of the covenant is the plain teaching of Psalm 89. "I have made a covenant with my chosen...My covenant shall stand fast with him" (Ps. 89:3, 28). Also Galatians 3:16 teaches that God established his covenant with Jesus Christ, the singular "seed" of Abraham, by covenant promise to him, as head of the covenant. Galatians 3:29 includes in this "seed" all those, but those only, who are "Christ's." They, and they only, are "heirs according to the promise" of the covenant, which promise God has made exclusively to Christ and to those baby boys and girls who are his by eternal election.

The doctrine of the unconditional covenant is the doctrine of a covenant that recognizes that God in his sovereign good

regard to the children of believers, see Engelsma, "The Covenant Doctrine of the Fathers of the Secession," in *Always Reforming*, 100–136; for Bavinck's covenant doctrine, see Herman Bavinck, *Reformed Dogmatics*, vol. 3, *Sin and Salvation in Christ*, ed. John Bolt, trans. John Vriend (Grand Rapids, MI: Baker, 2006), 196–232; for Hoeksema's doctrine of the covenant, see Herman Hoeksema, *Believers and Their Seed: Children in the Covenant* (Grandville, MI: Reformed Free Publishing Association, rev. ed. 1997).

pleasure makes distinction between two kinds of physical offspring of believing parents. As Romans 9:6 teaches, some children of believers are merely "of Israel," whereas others are "Israel." Some are merely under the administration of the covenant, or in the sphere of the covenant, greatly aggravating the guilt of their wicked unbelief and disobedience. Others—the elect, the children of the promise—*are God's Israel*, that is, God's covenant friends by union with Christ on the basis of the cross.

The doctrine of the unconditional covenant is the doctrine of a covenant that is established and maintained by a covenant promise that is sure to all the seed of Abraham. Not one, therefore, who has been united to Christ, who has believed on Christ from the heart, and who has been justified will ever fall away and perish. "[Covenant salvation] is of faith, that it might be by grace; to the end the promise might be sure to all the seed" (Rom. 4:16). This is Calvinism's precious assurance of salvation, *in and with regard to the covenant*, an assurance utterly destroyed by the federal vision.

The doctrine of the unconditional covenant is the doctrine of a covenant that confesses, on the basis of Jeremiah 31:31–34, that the faith and obedience of covenant children are God's gifts to them, in fulfillment of the covenant promise to them, not conditions upon which God's promise and their salvation shakily depend. "I will make a new covenant with the house of Israel...[and] I will put my law in their inward parts, and write it in their hearts" (vv. 31, 33).

THE SLANDER OF ANTINOMIANISM

Against this doctrine of the unconditional covenant will be lodged a vehement objection: "Denial of the responsibility of man!" "Luther's contempt for the law of God!" (A slander of Luther, formerly wickedly made against that great man of God by the Roman Catholic foes of his gospel of grace, now eagerly echoed by the men of the federal vision.) "Antinomian!"

This is always the objection of the enemies of grace against the proclamation of the gospel of salvation by grace alone. The enemies of grace raised the objection against Paul: Your gospel amounts to teaching, "Let us do evil, that good may come" (Rom. 3:8); your teaching makes "void the law" (v. 31); you encourage people to "continue in sin, that grace may abound" (Rom. 6:1).

Rome raised the objection against the gospel of grace confessed by the Reformation, as the Heidelberg Catechism indicates in question and answer 64. With specific reference to the doctrine of justification by faith alone, apart from any good work and all good works of the sinner—the truth that is a stone of stumbling and rock of offense to the federal vision—the Catechism hears the Roman Catholic Church objecting: "But does not this doctrine make men careless and profane?"[13]

It is extraordinarily significant that the men of the federal vision and their supporters charge the gospel of grace *in its application to the covenant* with antinomianism. In effect, and sometimes explicitly, they charge that the doctrine of the unconditional covenant is antinomian.

Norman Shepherd insists that a doctrine of a conditional covenant is necessary in order to ward off the dread evil of antinomianism. A doctrine of an unconditional covenant is antinomian. Only because it is conditional, according to Norman Shepherd, the "Abrahamic covenant cannot give comfort to the antinomians."[14]

Richard B. Gaffin Jr. explains Romans 2:13 ("the doers of the law shall be justified") "as describing what will be true of Christians at the final judgment,"[15] that is, the decisive justification of the final judgment will take into account the good works of Christians.

Denying that justification in James 2 is different from justification in Romans 3–5, Gaffin, in his characteristically dense and difficult style, makes as plain as he cares to that obedience

---

13   Heidelberg Catechism, Q. 64, in *Creeds of Christendom*, 3:328.

14   Shepherd, *Call of Grace*, 22.

15   Richard B. Gaffin Jr., *By Faith, Not By Sight: Paul and the Order of Salvation* (Bletchley, Milton Keynes, Bucks, UK: Paternoster, 2006), 97.

is essential to the justification of the sinner that Paul teaches in Romans 3–5, particularly with regard to Abraham: "The Abraham of the obedience of faith implicitly brackets and so qualifies everything Paul says about him and his faith...in Romans."[16] When Paul says about Abraham and his faith, in Romans 4:5, that Abraham did not work for justification, but only believed; that in the moment of justification Abraham was an ungodly man; and that Abraham's faith was counted for Abraham's righteousness—all of this must be "bracketed" and "qualified" by "the Abraham of the obedience of faith."

Bracketing and qualifying Romans 4:5 with the Abraham of the obedience of faith, according to the exegetical directive of Richard Gaffin, we must now understand Romans 4:5 thus: "To him [Abraham] who did not give up working, but was obedient, and believed on Him who does not justify ungodly persons, but persons [like Abraham] who are obedient (of course, with the obedience of faith), his faith, that is, *an obedient, working faith*, is counted for righteousness."

Gaffin tells us the reason for this cautious and carefully, even oddly, worded—but unmistakable—criticism of justification by faith alone, altogether apart from good works, and thus attack on the gospel of salvation by grace alone. It is his fear, amounting to the charge, that by their doctrine of justification by faith alone, the churches of the Reformation fail to do justice to sanctification. This failure is "pervasive."[17]

Rome was right, according to Richard Gaffin, in its charge against the Reformation that the Reformation's gospel of grace, particularly its doctrine of justification by faith alone, did not do justice to a life of sanctification and good works.

The claim of the men of the federal vision that they are motivated to deny justification by faith alone and sovereign grace in the covenant because of the evil of antinomianism, of which these doctrines supposedly are the cause, is spread

16   Ibid., 104.
17   Ibid., 76.

abroad on the back cover of *The Auburn Avenue Theology*: "rampant antinomianism in contemporary Christianity."

Federal vision sympathizer P. Andrew Sandlin is blunt and vehement: "To preach that the covenant is unconditional is to preach an antinomian gospel, false to its very core."[18]

By this charge, we defenders of the unconditional covenant—the covenant of *grace*—are encouraged.

The gospel of grace is always assailed as antinomian. The charge against a theology that it is antinomian is virtually the seal upon it that it is, as it claims to be, the systematizing of the gospel of grace of Holy Scripture.

The charge is false. It is a slander. The response to it, in every age, by the defender of grace is the apostle's "God forbid" (Rom. 3:31; Rom. 6:1–2). The same gospel that freely justifies sanctifies powerfully. The Holy Spirit causes the justified sinner to love God and the neighbor in thankfulness for the free pardon of sins on the ground of the death of Jesus Christ.[19]

But if a theology does not draw the charge "antinomian!" it ought to examine itself whether it is faithful to the gospel of grace. If a theology *of the covenant* does not draw the charge "antinomian," it should examine itself whether it magnifies the grace of God in Jesus Christ.

Who would ever dream of charging the federal vision and its doctrine of a conditional covenant with antinomianism? The

---

18 Sandlin, "Covenant in Redemptive History: 'Gospel and Law' or 'Trust and Obey'?," in *Backbone of the Bible*, 83.

19 Gaffin has his doubts also about the Reformation's and the Reformed creeds' teaching concerning sanctification. Spirit-worked gratitude for gracious justification is not enough to produce a life of good works, as, of course, is the teaching about the Christian life by the third part of the Heidelberg Catechism. Something more, something other, is needed to motivate Christians. That something is "bracketing" and "qualifying" everything Paul teaches about justification in Romans 3–5 with the *obedience* of faith. Gaffin deplores the tendency of Reformed Christians to see "sanctification...as the response of the believer to salvation, defined in terms of justification. Sanctification [mistakenly, according to Gaffin] is viewed as an expression of gratitude from our side for our justification and the free forgiveness of our sins, usually with the accent on the imperfection and inadequacy of such expressions of gratitude" (*By Faith, Not By Sight*, 76).

covenant doctrine of the federal vision fairly bristles with conditions, works, and law, from beginning to end and from top to bottom. Not only does it bristle with law, it makes obedience to the law the ground—*condition!*—of salvation in the covenant. It would never enter one's mind to allege against one of the proponents of the federal vision, "You make void the law."

The charge against the federal vision is that it makes void the gospel.

Inasmuch as the Reformation was Christ's restoration of the gospel of grace to his church, the federal vision is the overthrow in conservative Reformed churches at the beginning of the twenty-first century of the sixteenth-century Reformation of the church.

Only by repudiating the federal vision at its root—the doctrine of a conditional covenant—and by confessing sovereign grace in the covenant—the doctrine of the unconditional covenant—do Reformed and Presbyterian churches and members truly commemorate, maintain, develop, and defend in the twenty-first century the sixteenth-century Reformation of the church.

THE GOSPEL OF THE REFORMATION AT ISSUE 5

Assurance of Salvation | The Glory of God

At issue in the controversy of Reformed orthodoxy with the federal vision at the beginning of the twenty-first century is the gospel of grace restored by Christ to the church in the Reformation of the sixteenth century, nothing less.

It is the privilege of Reformed and Presbyterian Christians and churches to celebrate that glorious work of the risen Jesus Christ in the history of his church.

It is the experience of Reformed and Presbyterian Christians and churches that they are thankful for it.

It is the calling of Reformed and Presbyterian Christians and churches to maintain the Reformation by confessing and proclaiming the grand truths the Reformation recovered and restored to the church: justification by faith alone; salvation by sovereign, particular grace alone; election as the source and foundation of all grace and salvation; Jesus Christ, the only, complete, sufficient, and effectual Savior.

In their maintenance of the Reformation, the Reformed churches are called to develop the truths of the Reformation. They must bring out more of the infinite riches of the revelation of God in Jesus Christ. They must more closely relate the various doctrines to each other. They must do justice to truths that hitherto have been somewhat neglected. They must increase in their understanding of all the truths. They must apply the truths more powerfully to the life of the believers and their children.

One important biblical doctrine in particular that needs development is that of the covenant. The reformers certainly had much to say about the covenant. But they did not develop this doctrine thoroughly and completely. Some of the earlier ministers in the Reformed tradition, for example Bullinger, corrupted the pure truth of the covenant. These impurities must be purged from the Reformed churches' conception of the covenant.

In all the development of the truths of the Reformation, particularly the truth of the covenant, genuine development will consist of faithfully applying the gospel's central message of salvation by sovereign grace to the truths. Whatever the doctrine may be, if the contemporary church's work with it ends in denying or even weakening sovereign grace, the work is not development, but deviation and departure.

Regarding the important work of development of doctrine too, the command is "hold the traditions which ye have been taught" (2 Thess. 2:15).

The Reformed churches are called to contend for the faith once delivered to the saints by the prophetic and apostolic word of Scripture and then restored at the Reformation. They must defend the gospel of grace against Roman Catholicism, liberal Protestantism, Arminianism, and the federal vision. Especially are Reformed churches to defend the gospel against the federal vision, since this is the real and present danger to the faith of the Reformation for Reformed and Presbyterian churches in our day. We remember the saying attributed to Luther, to the effect that the man or the church that defends all of the truth except the one doctrine that is presently under attack has in fact denied the faith in its entirety.

The federal vision is the enemy of the Reformation. It is the enemy of the Reformation *within the gates* and, therefore, the most dangerous enemy of all. It is obviously and undeniably the enemy of the Reformation, for it teaches justification by faith and works. Thus it denies the heart of the Reformation gospel and, therefore, the entire Reformation gospel of grace.

By its rejection of justification by faith alone—*in the covenant, and as fruit of its doctrine of a conditional covenant*—the federal vision opposes and subverts the Reformation with regard to the two main purposes of the Reformation.

ASSURANCE OF SALVATION

One main purpose of the Reformation was the assurance of salvation of every believer and every true, spiritual child of believers. Every believer can have, ought to have, has the right to have, and will have assurance of salvation. True faith *is* assurance of salvation. "What is true faith?" the great Catechism of the Reformation asked of every believer, weak as well as strong, young as well as old, newly converted as well as long established in the truth. Into the mouth of every believer, including the spiritual child of the believer, the Catechism placed this answer: "not only a certain knowledge...*but also a hearty trust which the Holy Ghost works in me by the Gospel, that not only to others, but to me also, forgiveness of sins, everlasting righteousness and salvation, are freely given by God, merely of grace, only for the sake of Christ's merits.*"[1]

As the Catechism indicates, this precious assurance of salvation is worked, not by every religious teaching that calls itself the Christian gospel, but by the gospel—the biblical good news of grace. Whatever is not the gospel works doubt of salvation.

The Catechism also makes clear that assurance of salvation rests squarely on the truth that forgiveness and righteousness, which are the two aspects of justification, and, therefore, salvation in its entirety are wholly the gift of pure grace, earned by and dependent upon the merits of Christ alone: "freely given by God, merely of grace, only for the sake of Christ's merits." Corrupt the truth of grace, make the righteousness of the sinner partly his own obedience, suspend salvation on conditions performed by the sinner, direct his trust in any way toward himself, and assurance of salvation is, thereby, destroyed.

The believer's assurance of salvation, according to the gospel of the Reformation, is by no means limited to certainty of present salvation. It is this, but it is far more than this. Assurance of

---

1 Heidelberg Catechism, Q&A 21, in *Creeds of Christendom*, 3:313; emphasis added.

present salvation might be claimed by one who, nevertheless, doubts whether he will be saved eternally, or even tomorrow. Many who do claim to be saved live in the fear that they may fall away and perish everlastingly. This is not assurance but doubt.

The comfort of the gospel of the Reformation is the certainty of God's gracious preservation of every believer in salvation. Of this every believer may be, and will be, assured. Therefore, he is assured of salvation in the everlasting future.

> Of this preservation of the elect to salvation, and of their perseverance in the faith, true believers for themselves may and do obtain assurance according to the measure of their faith, whereby they arrive at the certain persuasion that they ever will continue true and living members of the Church; and that they experience forgiveness of sins, and will at last inherit eternal life.[2]

As this statement of the believer's confidence concerning his preservation suggests, the foundation of assurance of salvation is God's eternal election as a gracious, that is, unconditional and therefore unchangeable, choice of the person. Of his election, that is, of his salvation in eternity past, every believer is assured by the gospel of the Reformation. "The elect, in due time, though in various degrees and in different measures, attain the assurance of this their eternal and unchangeable election."[3]

This assurance of salvation is inseparably bound up with the gospel of justification by faith alone, apart from works, and with the gospel of salvation by grace alone, of which justification by faith alone is an essential aspect. The Spirit bears witness with the spirit of one who hears and believes the gospel of sovereign grace of the epistle to the Romans that he is a child of God (Rom. 8:16). No one else has this witness. The man or woman who is righteous before God by faith alone is certain that nothing shall separate him or her from the love of Christ (v. 35). No one else has this certainty.

2   Canons of Dordt, 5.9, in ibid., 3:594.
3   Canons of Dordt, 1.12, in ibid., 3:583.

The Reformation excoriated Rome for casting all its members into doubt about their salvation by its doctrine of justification by faith and good works. The Belgic Confession had the doctrine of Rome in view when it warned what the result must be of founding one's salvation upon his own good works, rather than upon "the merits of the suffering and death of our Saviour": "Thus, then, we should always be in doubt, tossed to and fro without any certainty, and our poor consciences would be continually vexed."[4] This is every Roman Catholic. This is every one who believes the false gospel of Arminianism. This is every one who sees covenant salvation with the sight of the federal vision.

"Always...in doubt, tossed to and fro without any certainty... poor consciences...continually vexed."

Like Rome and like Arminianism, the federal vision warns every member of the covenant that, even though he shares in the "initial" grace that will assist in bringing others to heaven, even though he believes in Christ, even though he is united to Christ by a living faith, and even though he is justified and enjoys other covenant blessings today, he can fall away from Christ, lose the grace of justification and salvation, and be damned tomorrow, and eternally.

The men of the federal vision are not cautious in their expression of the possibility of falling away. The reality of the apostasy of covenant saints is one of their favorite doctrines. Here they outdo the early Arminians. Prior to Dordt, the Arminians were very careful in putting forward their teaching of the falling away of saints. When pressed, they would say only that they could not commit themselves on the doctrine of perseverance, one way or the other.

> Whether they [those who are incorporated into Jesus Christ and thereby become partakers of his life-giving Spirit] can through negligence fall away from the first principle of their life in Christ, again embrace the

4   Belgic Confession, Art. 24, in ibid., 3:412.

present world, depart from the pure doctrine once given to them, lose the good conscience, and neglect grace, must first be more carefully determined from the Holy Scriptures before we shall be able to teach this with the full persuasion of our heart.[5]

The Arminians had good reason for their caution. They knew full well the biblical teaching of God's faithful preservation of all those whom he gave to Christ in the decree of election.

My sheep hear my voice, and I know them, and they follow me: And I give unto them eternal life; and they shall never perish, neither shall any man pluck them out of my hand. My Father, which gave them me, is greater than all; and no man is able to pluck them out of my Father's hand (John 10:27–29).

The Arminians were well aware also of the terror that their doctrine of the falling away of the saints must strike into the hearts of all believers.

The federal vision in contrast is bold, recklessly bold, showing no regard for the faithfulness and power of God or for the peace of believers.

God gave them [those in the sphere of the covenant who fall away and perish everlastingly—baptized children of believers] genuine promises that are just as real, just as dependable, and just as trustworthy as the promises he gave to people who do persevere to the end. He gave them real promises of salvation. He united them to Christ in whom alone there is salvation, and they themselves really rejected it because they didn't receive the promises mixed with faith.[6]

5 "The Remonstrance of 1610/5," in *Crisis in the Reformed churches: Essays in commemoration of the great Synod of Dort, 1618-1619*, ed. Peter Y. De Jong (Grand Rapids, MI: Reformed Fellowship, 1968), 209.

6 John Barach, *Covenant!*, audio tapes of lectures by John Barach, Steve Wilkins, Steve Schlissel, and Douglas Wilson presented at the 2002 Pastors' Conference, Auburn Avenue Presbyterian Church, Monroe, LA (Brooklyn: Messiah's Ministries, 2002).

Those who ultimately prove to be reprobate may be in covenant with God. They may enjoy for a season the blessings of the covenant, including the forgiveness of sins, adoption, possession of the kingdom, sanctification, etc., and yet apostatize and fall short of the grace of God...*The apostate doesn't forfeit "apparent blessings" that were never his in reality, but real blessings that were his in covenant with God.*[7]

Clearly, then, Hebrews 6:4–8 teaches the possibility of a real apostasy. Some people do indeed fall away, and it is a *real* fall *from* grace. Apostates actually lose blessings they once possessed. Apostasy is so terribly heinous precisely because it is sin against grace.[8]

The federal vision is a theology of doubt.

It is a theology of doubt for the same reason that every other false gospel that teaches the terrifying doctrine of the falling away of saints is a theology of doubt: a doctrine of conditional grace and conditional salvation. In the case of the federal vision, the heretical doctrine takes the form of conditional grace and salvation *in the covenant*. The federal vision *tells* the Reformed churches and members that the reason for its doctrine of the "real" falling away of covenant saints is its doctrine of a conditional covenant.

God truly brings those people into His covenant, into union with Christ. They are "in Him," to use Jesus' words in John 15. They share in His blessings (think of Hebrews 6). They experience His love, *but that covenant relationship is conditional. It calls for repentance and faith and new obedience. God's choice was not conditional, but life in the covenant is.*[9]

7 Wilkins, "Covenant, Baptism, and Salvation," in *Auburn Avenue Theology*, 264; the emphasis is Wilkins'.

8 Lusk, "New Life and Apostasy: Hebrews 6:4–8 as Test Case," in *Federal Vision*, 274; the emphasis is Lusk's.

9 Barach, "Covenant and Election," in ibid., 37; emphasis added.

Doubt about salvation—the terror of the possibility of falling away from Christ and of losing salvation—is contrary to the gracious will of the covenant God for his children, including his little, childish children. He does not will that we live and die in the terror of the possibility of falling away. He does not will that Reformed parents and grandparents, who believe the covenant promise and, therefore, rear their children and grandchildren in the nurture and admonition of the Lord, toss and turn on their beds at night, worrying themselves sick about the salvation of their children and grandchildren.

> If the elect of God were deprived of this solid comfort, that they shall finally obtain the victory, and of this infallible pledge or earnest of eternal glory, they would be of all men the most miserable.[10]

God wills the comfort of his chosen people. This comfort includes the "assur[ance]…of eternal life."[11]

The gospel of the Reformation gives this comfort.

THE GLORY OF GOD

The second main purpose of the Reformation, and not the lesser, was the glory of God. "To God alone the glory!"—this was one of the great *solas* (onlys) of the Reformation. This was not for the reformers and their congregations, and may not become for us, a meaningless, hypocritical cliché. As Ephesians 1:6 ("to the praise of the glory of his grace") and Romans 11:36 ("to whom be glory for ever") declare, the glory of the triune God in Jesus Christ is the ultimate purpose of God with salvation. And this glory of God is his saving of the elect church by grace—free, sovereign, particular, unconditional grace.

This burning purpose of the Reformation is strikingly evident in the Canons of Dordt, which defend and confess the gospel of the Reformation at its heart—the message of salvation by sovereign, particular, free, unconditional grace. Every one of

---

10   Canons of Dordt, 5.10, in *Creeds of Christendom*, 3:594.

11   Heidelberg Catechism, A. 1, in ibid., 3:308.

the positive heads of doctrine concludes with a doxology. Only one who is ignorant of the mind of the synod could attribute this to accident. By the mind of the synod, the Holy Spirit, who guided the synod in a special way, leading the church into all truth, thus expressed the end, or goal, of the truths of the gospel confessed in all the heads of doctrine.

The first head, on unconditional election, concludes thus: "'Of him, and through him, and to him are all things: to whom be glory forever. Amen.' (Rom. 11:33–36.)"[12]

The second head, on the effectual death of Christ for the elect and for the elect only, thus confirming the covenant with them, concludes this way: "and which [the elect church for whom Christ died] may celebrate his praises here and through all eternity."[13]

The third and fourth heads, on the regeneration of, conversion of, and gift of faith to the elect by irresistible, or sovereign, grace, conclude thus: "to whom [God] alone all the glory, both of means and their saving fruit and efficacy, is forever due. Amen."[14]

The fifth head, on God's preservation of the saints so that they persevere in holiness and salvation, concludes thus: "NOW TO THIS ONE GOD, FATHER, SON, AND HOLY SPIRIT BE HONOR AND GLORY FOREVER. AMEN."[15]

The literature of the federal vision breathes nothing of this one, grand purpose. The theology of the federal vision is of, through, and unto what the men of the federal vision would call the "responsibility of man" in the covenant. In fact, its great concern is not the truth of man's responsibility. Its concern, rather, is to establish the *sovereignty* of man in the covenant.

That man or woman glorifies God who ascribes all of his or her salvation, *in the covenant*, to the grace of God, and to the grace of God only.

That church glorifies God that proclaims the gospel of salvation by sovereign grace, and by sovereign grace only, *in the covenant*.

12 Canons of Dordt, 1.18, in ibid., 3:585.

13 Canons of Dordt, 2.9, in ibid., 3:587.

14 Canons of Dordt, 3–4.17, in ibid., 3:592.

15 Canons of Dordt, 5.15, in ibid., 3:595.

The federal vision robs God of his glory—a sin than which there is no sin greater—just as the Roman Catholic Church did at the time of the Reformation, and does still today, and just as Arminianism did at the time of Dordt, and does still today. The federal vision gives the glory of salvation to the child who performs the decisive conditions.

In the theology of the federal vision, covenant election depends upon the child's performing the conditions of the covenant.

In the theology of the federal vision, the efficacy of the cross for covenant redemption depends upon the child's performing the conditions of the covenant.

In the theology of the federal vision, the fulfillment of the covenant promise depends upon the child's performing the conditions of the covenant.

In the theology of the federal vision, the maintaining of the covenant bond with Christ and the continuing of covenant grace and covenant blessings depend upon the child's performing the conditions of the covenant.

In the theology of the federal vision, final, everlasting, covenant salvation depends upon the child's performing the conditions of the covenant.

The men of the federal vision cannot object against this critique of their theology, that the child performs all the conditions with the help of the grace of God, for in the theology of the federal vision covenant grace is *resistible*, not sovereign. All the performing of the conditions, therefore, in the end *depends on the will and working of the child.*

Loath as the men of the federal vision are to state openly the implication of their covenant theology—understandably so—their theology of covenant salvation ends in glorifying the covenant child for saving himself, or for allowing God to save him, which is the same thing.

The federal vision robs God of his glory in the greatest of his works.

Every Reformed and Presbyterian theologian and church that approves, or tolerates, or simply refuses to condemn the federal vision doctrine of a conditional covenant connives at the robbing of God of his glory, in covenant salvation, and at the robbing of the covenant people of God of the assurance of covenant salvation.

They are warned!

At bottom, the issue raised by the federal vision is simple, though profound. Is God dependent upon the sinner, or is the sinner dependent upon God? Is God dependent upon the sinner—a baptized, sinful infant—regarding *salvation in the covenant*, or is the sinner, *in the covenant*, dependent upon God for *salvation in the covenant*?

A god dependent upon the sinner is not the God of the Reformed faith. It is not the true, living God of Christianity and of the Bible. It is an idol.

As for me, and the churches in which I am a minister of the gospel, our confession is this: Of God—*in the covenant*—and through God—*in the covenant*—and unto God—*in the covenant*—are all things—concerning our salvation *in the covenant*; to whom be glory—for the salvation of us and our children *in the covenant*—forever. Amen.

PART 2

*Answers to Questions
about the Federal Vision and
the Covenant of Grace*

INTRODUCTION TO PART 2

At the several deliverances of the lecture that has been reworked and expanded to form the first part of this book, the audiences had questions. These questions I answer in the second part of *Federal Vision*.

Many of the questions sincerely seek instruction. Some challenge the criticism of the federal vision and its advocates. A few are hostile. All express genuine concerns of Reformed and Presbyterian church members regarding the federal vision. Lectures and books address concerns that speakers and authors think that audiences and readers *ought* to have. Answers to questions address concerns that people *do* have.

The answers in the second part of the book to the many, wide-ranging questions shed more light on the theology of the federal vision—its nature; its main tenets; its origins; its powerful proponents in the Reformed and Presbyterian churches; its handling of Scripture and the creeds; and, not least, its dreadful effects on those deceived by it.

I welcomed these questions, hostile as well as friendly.

They afforded, and now, as part of the book, continue to afford, further opportunity to root out the federal vision on behalf of the covenant of grace.

THE FEDERAL VISION, ITS DOCTRINES, AND ITS DEFENDERS 6

Would you give a short definition of what federal vision is? Where did this name come from? Why is this theology and movement called federal vision?

The federal vision is a recent heresy in some of the most prominent and influential conservative Presbyterian and Reformed denominations and congregations in North America.

It is a theology and movement that explicitly denies the fundamental truth of the gospel recovered by the sixteenth-century Reformation of the church, that is, justification by faith alone. With this central gospel truth, the federal vision also explicitly denies all the doctrines of salvation by sovereign, particular grace, popularly known as the five points of Calvinism and officially adopted by the Reformed churches in the Canons of Dordt and by the Presbyterian churches in the Westminster standards.

The federal vision denies these truths *with specific reference to salvation in the covenant.*

This explains its name.

Federal vision is the name by which the leading proponents of the theology and movement themselves call their theology and movement. It is the name they themselves have chosen for themselves.

The name is well chosen.

The federal vision is essentially a doctrine and corresponding practice of the covenant. "Federal," derived from the Latin *foedus*, means covenant.

The federal vision at its root is a doctrine of the covenant that holds that God establishes his covenant with all the physical, baptized children of believing parents alike, uniting them all alike to Christ in the same gracious, spiritual manner, according to his gracious, covenant promise to all alike. But (according to the federal vision) the covenant, the covenant promise, covenant grace, covenant blessings, and covenant salvation are *conditional*. The maintenance of the covenant with the children, the continued enjoyment of covenant blessings (including especially justification) by the children, and the fulfillment of the covenant promise to the children in their everlasting salvation depend upon decisions the children must make and works the children must do. These conditions are faith, repentance, good works, and, generally, lifelong covenant faithfulness.

One aspect of this covenant doctrine, which the men of the federal vision emphasize, is that boys and girls, men and women, can and do fall away from covenant grace and salvation; can and do separate themselves from Christ, to whom once they were truly, spiritually united; can and do lose the grace of justification, which once they possessed. In the language of Reformed theology, the federal vision teaches the falling away of saints—*in the covenant and with regard to covenant salvation.*

The federal vision, by its own, open acknowledgment, is the development of the covenant doctrine of the Reformed Churches in the Netherlands (liberated) and their daughter churches, for instance, the Canadian Reformed Churches. It is the covenant doctrine of Klaas Schilder, Benne Holwerda, and Cornelis Veenhof in full, logical, necessary, inevitable development.

In simple laymen's terms, what is the definition of the root of the federal vision? Keep it plain.

I described the root of the heresy of the federal vision in simple laymen's terms in my lecture. I quote from my manuscript, which I deliberately wrote out in full for the lecture and deliberately followed carefully as I gave the lecture. I also deliberately phrased the entire lecture in the "simple" language of the layman, rather than in the characteristic language of the theologian, because I was, and am, mainly intent on reaching the believing members of the Reformed churches, not only of the Protestant Reformed Churches, but also of the other conservative Reformed and Presbyterian churches. The ministers in those churches know, or should know, the root of the federal vision. But these members are not being told the root of the federal vision and, therefore, the truth of that heretical theology. I was, and am, determined that the truth of the federal vision come home to the laymen in "simple" language, so that some of them might be convinced of the utter gravity of the presence of this contemporary heresy in their midst and take appropriate action and so that the others might be left without excuse.

Here is what I said about the root of the federal vision according to my manuscript, which is before me.

"Tonight...I expose the *root* of the federal vision. The federal vision is a theology of the *covenant*—a body of teachings about the *covenant*. This is what the federal vision is *fundamentally*... And what *is* the distinctive covenant doctrine of the federal vision? What *is* its supposedly new vision regarding the covenant of God in Christ? What *is* this covenant doctrine that manifests itself in the teaching of justification by works? in the teaching of an election of many unto grace and salvation in time that nevertheless fails to assure their eternal salvation? in the teaching of a saving grace that can be resisted and lost? in the teaching of the falling away of many into hell who once truly believed and enjoyed union with Christ?

"The federal vision's distinctive doctrine of the covenant is that the covenant is *conditional*: the covenant of God depends upon us humans—upon us with whom God establishes his covenant; because the federal vision is especially a doctrine of the covenant with regard to the baptized babies of believers, the covenant doctrine of the federal vision is that the covenant depends upon the baptized infants...

"What exactly and simply *is* the doctrine of a conditional covenant as it is now fully developed by the federal vision?

"It is the teaching that God on his part is gracious to all the baptized babies of believing members of the church alike, but that whether this grace abides with a child and is effective to bring a child to everlasting salvation in Abraham's bosom depends upon conditions that the child must perform (the conditions being the child's faith and obedience); some children perform the conditions and are saved; others—many others—fail to perform the conditions and go lost, despite the fact that God was as gracious to them as he was to those who are saved."

I then "simply" mentioned certain details of the conditional covenant doctrine of the federal vision, particularly concerning the baptized babies of godly parents. Again, I quote from my lecture.

"Covenant grace...according to the federal vision is conditional—from beginning to end it is conditional; it depends for its saving efficacy upon works that the child must do...The gracious attitude of God toward all the baptized babies alike is conditional; the covenant union with Christ established at baptism is conditional; enjoyment of all the covenant blessings, including justification, is conditional; everlasting covenant salvation in the new world is conditional."

Determined as I was to make the issue of the controversy of the Reformed faith with the root of the federal vision plain to every man, woman, and child in the audience of my lecture (while at the same time hoping to enlighten and encourage ministers who might be present), I concluded the lecture with yet another "simple" statement of the fundamental issue. Once more, I quote from my lecture as I wrote it in the manuscript.

"At bottom, the issue raised by the federal vision is simple... Is God dependent upon the sinner, or is the sinner dependent upon God? Is God dependent upon the sinner—a baptized, sinful infant—regarding *salvation in the covenant*, or is the sinner, *in the covenant*, dependent upon God for *salvation in the covenant*?"

Lest there yet be any failure to grasp the very heart of the root of the controversy, I then added: "A god dependent upon the sinner is not the God of the Reformed faith! It is not the true, living God of Christianity and of the Bible! It is an *idol!*" I may sum up this "simple" and "plain" description of the root of the federal vision with this simple definition. The root of the federal vision is the doctrine that the covenant of God in Christ is graciously established at baptism with all the physical children of believing parents alike, by gracious promise to all of them alike, but that the continuation of the covenant with a child, so that the child is saved everlastingly, depends upon works that the child must perform. To say it even more simply: The root of the federal vision is the doctrine of a gracious, but conditional, covenant with all the baptized children of believers alike, established by a gracious, but conditional, promise to all the children alike. To say it still more simply: The root of the federal vision is conditional, resistible grace in the covenant.

Where can we find federal vision proponents "openly and expressly" denying the five points of Calvinism?

For the attack on all the doctrines of sovereign grace by the men of the federal vision in their own writings, the concerned Reformed man or woman should read the following: Norman Shepherd, *The Call of Grace: How the Covenant Illuminates Salvation and Evangelism* (P&R, 2000); *The Auburn Avenue Theology, Pros & Cons: Debating the Federal Vision* (Knox Theological Seminary, 2004); *The Federal Vision*, ed. Steve Wilkins and Duane Garner (Athanasius Press, 2004); and *A Faith That Is Never Alone: A Response to Westminster Seminary California*, ed. P. Andrew Sandlin (Kerygma Press, 2007).

I demonstrated the charge that the men of the federal vision openly and expressly deny the five points of Calvinism in my book *The Covenant of God and the Children of Believers: Sovereign Grace in the Covenant*. The demonstration consists of an abundance of quotations from the writings and other utterances of the advocates of the federal vision.

Here I give representative statements by men of the federal vision denying the cardinal doctrines of the gospel of salvation by (sovereign) grace alone.

DENIAL OF JUSTIFICATION BY FAITH ALONE

"Romans 3:28 does not use the word 'alone,' when it speaks of justification by faith. Luther inserted this word into the translation of his German Bible because he thought it necessary to tweak [sic] the inspired word of God so that it would clearly say what he thought it ought to say...[The insertion of 'alone' is a] Lutheran gloss...'Works of the law' [in Romans 3:28]... are not simply any and all good works...By 'works of the law' Paul is referring to the old covenant...In Romans 3 Paul is not now teaching...that...*faith without faithfulness* is the real key to justification after all." "Justifying faith is a living and active, penitent faith."[1]

"To insist on faith alone for justification is a serious impoverishment."[2]

"[Paul] says in Romans 2:13 that in the Day of Judgment 'it is those who obey the law who will be declared righteous.' This is...justification by faith...faith that works...We are justified by living and active faith."[3]

"[Our good] works [are] a *condition* of final justification." "The works that justify at the last day are the works that flow out of a faith that has already received initial acceptance." "Final justification is by faith and works together." "In the final installment of our justification, there is a very real sense in which works will be the *decisive* factor."[4]

DENIAL OF ELECTION

Steve Wilkins has written that every baptized person is an elect in the sense that Ephesians 1:4 and 2 Thessalonians 2:13 teach election. Wilkins added: "[If baptized persons] later reject the Savior, they are no longer elect—they are cut off from the

1   Shepherd, "Faith and Faithfulness," in *A Faith That Is Never Alone*, 65–68.

2   Shepherd, "The Relation of Good Works to Justification in the Westminster Standards," cited in Downes, *Risking the Truth*, 137.

3   Shepherd, "Faith and Faithfulness," in *A Faith That Is Never Alone*, 66.

4   Lusk, "Future Justification: Some Theological and Exegetical Proposals," in ibid., 342–43, 354, 318; the emphasis is Lusk's.

Elect One and thus lose their elect standing. But their falling away doesn't negate the reality of their standing prior to their apostasy. They were really and truly the elect of God because of their relationship to Christ."[5]

"In Ephesians 1[:4], Paul writes from the perspective of observable covenant reality and concludes from the visible faith and sanctity of the Ephesians that they are the elect of God...It is true that some in the congregation may fall away and leave the church...Were some to fall away, he would no longer speak of them as the elect of God."[6]

"We should not drive a wedge between 'special' and 'covenantal' elections, for special election simply is covenantal election for those, who by God's sovereign electing grace, persevere. *For those who fall away, covenantal election devolves into reprobation.*"[7]

DENIAL OF LIMITED ATONEMENT

Having criticized the "Calvinist" interpretation of John 3:16, which insists that the "saving love of God revealed in the atonement is only for the elect," Shepherd declares, "The Reformed evangelist can and must preach to everyone on the basis of John 3:16, 'Christ died to save you.'"[8]

"[Reprobates] experience the love of God—real love...On the basis of John 3:16, we can also say, 'God loves you [to unbelieving reprobates].'"[9] Frame expresses his indebtedness to Norman Shepherd for suggesting to him that God loves all who are in the sphere of the covenant, the Esaus as well as the Jacobs, with the love of John 3:16, that is, the love that gives Jesus Christ for the objects of the divine love.[10]

---

5   Wilkins, "Covenant, Baptism, and Salvation," in *Auburn Avenue Theology*, 261.

6   Shepherd, *Call of Grace*, 87–88.

7   Joel Garver, cited approvingly by Douglas Wilson, in *"Reformed" Is Not Enough*, 140–41; emphasis added.

8   Shepherd, *Call of Grace*, 84–85.

9   John Frame, *The Doctrine of God* (Phillipsburg: NJ, P&R, 2002), 418–19.

10 Ibid., 419.

DENIAL OF IRRESISTIBLE (EFFICACIOUS) GRACE

All the baptized children of believers, those who perish as well as those who are saved everlastingly, receive "the same initial grace."[11]

"Covenant members [who will eventually fall away and perish] are actually brought to Christ, united to Him and the Church in baptism, receive various gracious operations of the Holy Spirit, and may even be said to be loved by God for a time...In some sense, they were really joined to the elect people, really sanctified by Christ's blood, and really recipients of new life given by the Holy Spirit. The sacraments they received had objective force and efficacy."[12]

"God truly brings those people [who eventually will fall away and perish] into His covenant, into union with Christ. They are 'in Him,' to use Jesus' words in John 15. They share in His blessings (think of Hebrews 6). They experience His love, but that covenant relationship is conditional. It calls for repentance and faith and new obedience. God's *choice* was not conditional, but life in the covenant is."[13]

DENIAL OF THE PERSEVERANCE OF SAINTS

"Those who ultimately prove to be reprobate may be in covenant with God. They may enjoy for a season the blessings of the covenant, including the forgiveness of sins, adoption, possession of the kingdom, sanctification, etc., and yet apostatize and fall short of the grace of God."[14]

"Clearly, then, Hebrews 6:4–8 teaches the possibility of a real apostasy. Some people do indeed fall away, and it is a *real* fall *from* grace. Apostates actually lose blessings they once

---

11   "Summary Statement [of the Auburn Avenue Presbyterian Church]...on the Covenant, Baptism, and Salvation," cited in White, "Covenant and Apostasy," in *Auburn Avenue Theology*, 214.

12   Lusk, "New Life and Apostasy," in *Federal Vision*, 288.

13   Barach, "Covenant and Election," in ibid., 37.

14   Wilkins, "Covenant, Baptism, and Salvation," in ibid., 62.

possessed. Apostasy is so terribly heinous precisely because it is sin against grace."[15] The doctrines of salvation by the (sovereign) grace of God, with justification at their heart, are one gospel. Deny one, especially justification, and you necessarily deny them all.

What is the stance of the advocates of the federal vision regarding the imputation of Christ's righteousness to our account?

At bottom, the position of the federal vision is that there is no imputation of the righteousness of Christ to the account of the believer. The federal vision is opposed to imputation. Some of its leading representatives are sarcastic in their dismissal of the creedal doctrine of the reckoning of the obedience of Christ to the account of the believing sinner. They speak of it as a shuffling around of accounts in heavenly record books. "Our righteous status is not a matter of God doing mental tricks or shuffling righteousness around heavenly ledgers; it is a matter of our concrete, personal relationship with Christ himself."[16]

The men of the federal vision particularly object to the teaching of the imputation of Christ's active obedience to the believer. That is, they teach that those who believe in Christ are forgiven their sins on the basis of the death of Christ (although this takes place only by faith and works), but most of them deny outright that God imputes Christ's active obedience to the believer. In Reformed theology, the distinction active and passive refers to Christ's lifelong obedience to the law of God (his active obedience) and to his obedience in suffering and dying (his passive obedience).

The reason for the federal vision's very strong opposition to the imputation of Christ's active obedience is that its proponents want the good works that the believer himself does to be his own active obedience and righteousness, especially in the final judgment. "[Our good] works [are] a *condition* of

15 Lusk, "New Life and Apostasy," in ibid., 274.

16 Lusk, "From Birmingham, With Love: 'Federal Vision' Postcards," in *A Faith That Is Never Alone*, 132.

final justification." "The works that justify at the last day are the works that flow out of...faith." "Final justification is by faith and works together." "In the final installment of our justification, there is a very real sense in which works will be the *decisive* factor."[17]

The rejection of imputation is the total destruction of creedal Reformed Christianity, that is, of the biblical gospel of grace. According to creedal Reformed Christianity, God imputed Adam's disobedience to the entire human race, Jesus only excepted; God imputed the guilt of the elect to Jesus Christ; and God imputes the obedience of Jesus Christ to the elect.

Whatever religion rejects imputation—this imputation—is not Reformed Christianity.

Some of the proponents of the federal vision are decisional regenerationists; others hold to presupposed regeneration. How can you say that both hold to the same view of the covenant?

There are minor differences among the various spokesmen of the federal vision. But in the fundamental elements of the covenant doctrine that calls itself the federal vision there is agreement. The covenant doctrine of the federal vision theology, and of all its recognized spokesmen, is that God graciously makes his covenant with every baptized child of believing parents alike at baptism and by the sacrament of baptism. This establishment of the covenant with every child at baptism and by the sacrament of baptism is the uniting of the child to Jesus Christ in a spiritual union, so that the life and benefits of Jesus Christ come to all the baptized children alike. All alike by baptism are in a living, spiritual relationship with Jesus Christ. The new life of Jesus Christ is in all the children alike.

Not all the men of the federal vision like to describe this union with Christ as regeneration. But since the Bible teaches that regeneration is the beginning of the new life of Christ in one by virtue of his or her union with Christ, the federal vision

---

17   Lusk, "Future Justification," in ibid., 342–43, 354, 318; the emphasis is Lusk's.

teaches that every child is regenerated at and by virtue of his or her baptism.

This is not decisional regeneration, for it happens in an infant when the infant is unconscious and cannot make a decision. Neither is it presupposed regeneration, for the men of the federal vision do not *suppose* that every child is spiritually united to Christ at baptism. They are *sure* of it, as sure as they are that the water of baptism has been sprinkled on the child.

The federal vision attributes this covenantally saving work to the sacrament of baptism, or to the Holy Spirit working necessarily, invariably, and, therefore, virtually automatically by the sacrament. Therefore, although they reject the charge because, after all, it is a Roman Catholic heresy, the federal vision teaches a form of baptismal regeneration—call it "baptismal covenant union with Christ." It is essentially the same as the Roman Catholic doctrine. All the children are united to Christ and saved—temporarily.

But this covenant established with all the baptized children alike can be annulled. The union with Christ can be severed. The child can lose the life and benefits of Christ that once he or she possessed. For the covenant established at baptism is conditional. If the child sometime in his or her life right up to the very end, at the moment of death, in fact, should fail to perform the conditions of the covenant, the child will fall away from Christ and perish. There is a falling away of covenant saints. There is a loss of covenant grace and salvation.

John Barach writes, "All those who are baptized are genuinely baptized *into Christ* (Galatians 3:27), are brought into Christ's body, the church (I Corinthians 12:13), and are members of God's covenant, at least until they are cut off, whether by Christ's church (excommunication) or directly by Christ (death as judgment)."[18]

Douglas Wilson teaches the same. "Water baptism is covenantally efficacious. It brings every person baptized into some

18 Barach, "Covenant and Election," in *Auburn Avenue Theology*, 150; emphasis is Barach's.

kind of an objective and living covenant relationship with Christ, whether the baptized person is elect or reprobate. Baptism is always to be taken by the one baptized as a sign and seal of his ingrafting into Christ...Therefore we can say that baptism is the laver of regeneration (Titus 3:5)."[19]

And Rich Lusk: "These non-elect covenant members are actually brought to Christ, united to Him and the Church in baptism, receive various gracious operations of the Holy Spirit, and may even be said to be loved by God for a time...In some sense, they were really joined to the elect people, really sanctified by Christ's blood, and really recipients of new life given by the Holy Spirit. The sacraments they received had objective force and efficacy."[20]

This doctrine is the federal vision's development of the very popular and widespread covenant doctrine that teaches that God graciously extends his covenant promise to all the children alike at their baptism and graciously establishes his covenant with all the children alike at baptism, but that the covenant promise and the covenant itself are conditional, depending for their fulfillment, maintenance, and perfection (in the children's everlasting salvation) upon conditions the children must perform.

The covenant doctrine of the men of the federal vision is characterized by the same grievous errors that characterize the Arminian heresy repudiated by the Canons of Dordt: saving grace that is wider than the decree of election (because the grace of God in Christ does not have its source in election); grace that is resistible and losable; the (terrifying) possibility of the falling away of those once truly united to Christ and thus saved; the dependency of God's grace and salvation upon conditions that sinners must perform.

The special feature of the federal vision is that it corrupts the doctrine of the covenant with these errors, particularly, the doctrine of the covenant of God with the children of believers.

19 Wilson, "Sacramental Efficacy in the Westminster Standards," in ibid., 242–43.
20 Lusk, "New Life and Apostasy," in *Federal Vision*, 288.

Would Douglas Wilson say that those who remain in the covenant prove their election?

What Douglas Wilson would *say* about this matter, I do not know. Douglas Wilson is more careful to approximate the language of orthodoxy in propounding and defending the theology of the federal vision than most of his colleagues and allies. This is not to his credit. It makes him more dangerous to the Reformed faith and to Reformed people. That his caution in laying out the theology of the federal vision, especially when it is under attack, does not indicate any difference with his more candid colleagues is evident from the fact that he does not condemn them. On the contrary, he cooperates with them fully and defends them. "Birds of a feather flock together."

Whatever Douglas Wilson might *say* about the relation of remaining in the covenant and election, this is his theology, as one of the most prominent and influential proponents of the federal vision: At baptism, God puts all the children in the covenant of grace. All are united to Jesus Christ. All begin to receive the new life of Christ, as the sap of the vine flows into the branches. All the children alike are the objects of the only election of God that really matters with regard to the covenant: an election in time, unto covenant grace. But this election is conditional. It is not, therefore, also an election unto (eternal) glory. It is an election merely unto the *way* of salvation. It is not also an election unto *salvation*. Only by performing the conditions of the covenant, *as long as he or she lives*, does a child make this election effective and lasting.

Douglas Wilson and the federal vision do not teach that performing the condition of remaining in the covenant *proves* election. They teach that performing the condition of remaining in the covenant *makes election effectual*. Covenant election is conditioned by the child's faith and faithfulness. Many children, according to Wilson, refuse to perform the covenant conditions and thereby render God's election of them null and void. Wilson has written that their election then turns into reprobation: "We should not drive a wedge between 'special' and 'covenantal' elections, for special election simply is covenantal election for those, who by God's sovereign, electing grace, persevere. For those who fall away, covenantal election devolves into reprobation."[21]

According to Douglas Wilson and the other men of the federal vision, God puts children into the covenant—all who are baptized. Whether they remain in the covenant depends on them.

When this teaching is exposed for the heresy that it is, Wilson is quick to assure his audience that those eternally chosen will surely be saved. The ignorant and gullible are satisfied with this vague appeal to an eternal decree.

Mistakenly!

For, first, the false teaching is maintained: The election that governs the covenant is conditional.

Second, whatever the eternal decree may be in the theology of Douglas Wilson, it does not function with regard to the covenant; covenant grace; covenant union with Christ; covenant preservation; and covenant salvation. The eternal decree of election does not govern the covenant in the theology of the federal vision. It does not determine with whom God establishes the covenant. It is not the sole fountain of covenant grace. It does not assure that God will perfect the covenant salvation of all with whom he begins this salvation.

The eternal decree of election, accompanied by the eternal decree of reprobation, is a dead letter in the theology of the federal vision. Changing the figure, it is a museum piece that the men of the federal vision dust off and display for a moment whenever critics make it hot for them. I get the impression that the men of the federal vision are scared to death of the eternal decree, if they do not detest it. For them, it is certainly not the glorious, living, precious, gracious will of God, from which flows all of our salvation in the covenant, that it is in Reformed theology and in the consciousness of the Reformed believer.

<hr />

21 Wilson, *"Reformed" Is Not Enough*, 140–41; Wilson is quoting another with approval.

Third, I have no doubt that, if one would carefully investigate Wilson's and the federal vision's doctrine of the eternal decree of election (to which the men of the federal vision on occasion pay lip service), he would discover that the eternal decree unto everlasting glory is conditioned by the child's rendering temporal, covenant election effectual. That is, for the federal vision the eternal decree unto glory depends upon a child's performing the conditions of the covenant.

The Canons of Dordt say this about the election of God that governs the covenant, covenant grace, covenant preservation, and covenant salvation:

> This election was not founded upon foreseen faith, and the obedience of faith, holiness, or any other good quality or disposition in man, as the prerequisite, cause, or condition on which it depended; but men are chosen to faith and to the obedience of faith, holiness, etc. Therefore election is the fountain of every saving good.[22]

This is Reformed orthodoxy. This is the biblical gospel of grace. But this is not the message of Douglas Wilson and the federal vision.

In addition, the Canons deny that there are "various decrees of election." They affirm, rather, that

> [there is] one and the same decree respecting all those who shall be saved both under the Old and New Testament; since the Scripture declares the good pleasure, purpose, and counsel of the divine will to be one, according to which he hath chosen us from eternity, both to grace and to glory, to salvation and the way of salvation, which he hath ordained that we should walk therein.[23]

---

22 Canons of Dordt, 1.9, in *Creeds of Christendom*, 3:583.

23 Canons of Dordt, 1.8, in ibid., 3:583.

You charge that Richard B. Gaffin Jr. of the Orthodox Presbyterian Church is a defender and promoter of the federal vision. I object to that charge and ask that you prove it.

I do indeed charge that among the defenders and promoters of the federal vision is Richard B. Gaffin Jr. of the Orthodox Presbyterian Church. I am surprised that anyone should question this charge. So evident has Gaffin made his defense and promotion of the federal vision that what the questioner (who is really a challenger) calls a charge is more an observation than a charge.

Richard Gaffin is one of the most influential and prominent theologians in the Orthodox Presbyterian Church, indeed, one of the most influential and prominent theologians among all reputedly conservative Presbyterian and Reformed theologians today. This makes his defense and promotion of the federal vision especially dangerous to the Reformed churches and the Reformed faith.

My grounds for the charge are the following. First, during the six or seven years that the faculty and board of Westminster Seminary in Philadelphia struggled over Norman Shepherd, because of his teaching of justification by faith and works, among the most ardent and determined defenders of Norman Shepherd and his heretical doctrine was Richard Gaffin.[24] He has never publicly confessed this sin before the entire Presbyterian and Reformed community of churches, which has been, and still is, torn, divided, and corrupted by the covenant doctrine that Norman Shepherd has let loose into this community.

Second, on the back cover of Norman Shepherd's book *The Call of Grace*, there is a glowing recommendation of the book by Richard B. Gaffin Jr.

24 See Robertson, *The Current Justification Controversy*; MacLeod, "A Painful Parting, 1977–1983: Justifying Justification," in *W. Stanford Reid: An Evangelical Calvinist in the Academy*; Elliott, *Christianity and Neo-Liberalism: The Spiritual Crisis in the Orthodox Presbyterian Church and Beyond*; and Godfrey, "Westminster Seminary, the Doctrine of Justification, and the Reformed Confessions," in *The Pattern of Sound Doctrine: Systematic Theology at the Westminster Seminaries.*

This lucid and highly readable study provides valuable instruction on what it means to live in covenant with God. God's covenant is the only way of life that fully honors both the absolute, all-embracing sovereignty of his saving grace and the full, uninhibited activity of his people. *The Call of Grace* should benefit anyone concerned about biblical growth in Christian life and witness.[25]

The *Call of Grace* is the playbook of the theology of the federal vision. It denies justification by faith alone and all the doctrines of grace (the five points of Calvinism). It is the book that unleashed the controversy over the federal vision upon the public arena of Reformed Christianity in North America.

Third, when sound, aggrieved members of the Orthodox Presbyterian Church (believing men and women, among whom was not a single professor of theology or minister!) brought charges against a teacher of the federal vision, the defender of the heretical teacher and the champion of his federal vision theology at the general assembly of the Orthodox Presbyterian Church was Richard Gaffin. If Gaffin's defense was not the main cause of the exoneration of the teacher of the federal vision and, thus, the approval by the Orthodox Presbyterian Church of the heresy, it was one of the main causes.[26]

Fourth, Gaffin himself teaches justification by works, the prominent, bitter fruit of the theology of the federal vision. According to Gaffin, the public, decisive justification of the final judgment will be based in part on the good works of believers themselves, not only on the obedience of Jesus Christ in their stead. In the verdict of the final judgment, God will take into account not only the lifelong obedience and atoning death of

25 Gaffin, back cover of Shepherd, *The Call of Grace.*

26 See Paul M. Elliott, *A Denomination in Denial: An Evaluation of the Report of the Committee to Study the Doctrine of Justification of the Orthodox Presbyterian Church* (Westminster, MD: Teaching the Word, 2006), 37–41; on the "Kinnaird Case" at the 2003 general assembly of the Orthodox Presbyterian Church and the role of Richard Gaffin in defending the federal vision theology of Kinnaird, see also John W. Robbins, *Companion to the Current Justification Controversy,* 53–58.

Jesus Christ, but also the sinner's own works of obedience to the law. Explaining Romans 2:13, "For not the hearers of the law are just before God, but the doers of the law shall be justified," Gaffin writes: "The broader biblical context suggests that the positive outcome in view in Romans 2:5ff., at least in verses 5–11, *if not verses 12–13 as well,* is best seen as describing what will be true of Christians at the final judgment."[27]

Whereas the reformers and the Reformation creeds explain Romans 2:13 as teaching what *would* be the case if men were justified by the law, but *cannot possibly* be the case since no one is able to do the law, that is, obey it perfectly, Gaffin explains the text as teaching what *will actually* be the case: Men and women will be justified by their doing of the law.

This is vintage federal vision theology.

It is also damnable, soul-destroying heresy. It sends men and women into the final judgment depending on their own good works for their justification.

Once in my ministry, I knew a pastor (who had abandoned the Reformed faith for the charismatic religion) who sent a young, female parishioner into her death with the assurance that he—the pastor—would raise her from the dead. Sending people into the final judgment trusting in their own works for a favorable verdict from Judge Christ is worse.

When I answered the question about Richard Gaffin at the lecture, I took the occasion to beseech all in the audience that they not enter the final judgment appealing for a favorable verdict from the bench on the basis of a single good work of their own, even though that good work was performed in the power of the Spirit of Christ. I make the same exhortation to the readers of this book.

Every human who appears in the final judgment trusting in his or her own good works will be condemned and damned—*on the basis of the good works he or she appeals to for righteousness.* For all our good works are imperfect, corrupted with sin, and, in the matter of righteousness with God, deserving only

27 Gaffin, *By Faith, Not By Sight*, 97; emphasis added.

of condemnation. Only the work of Jesus Christ for us and outside us is perfect and both intended and prepared by God himself to be all our righteousness with him. We have this righteousness by faith alone, both now and in the final judgment. This points to the seriousness of the controversy of Reformed orthodoxy with the federal vision: The federal vision is sending people who profess to be, and probably think they are, Reformed and Presbyterian Christians into the final judgment to be condemned. For "by the deeds of the law there shall no flesh be justified in his sight" (Rom. 3:20).

But why can not our good works be the whole or part of our righteousness before God [now, or in the final judgment]?

Because the righteousness which can stand before the judgment-seat of God must be perfect throughout, and wholly conformable to the divine law; whereas even our best works in this life are all imperfect and defiled with sin.[28]

---

28 Heidelberg Catechism, Q&A 62, in *Creeds of Christendom*, 3:327.

THE FEDERAL VISION
AND CONDITIONS 7

What are some of the conditions a baptized child must perform to gain assurance of his salvation, according to the federal vision?

First, I correct the question. The federal vision does not merely teach that a baptized child must perform conditions to gain the *assurance* of salvation. It teaches that every baptized child must perform conditions to be *saved* in the covenant. According to the federal vision, God graciously begins the work of covenant salvation by uniting every child to Christ at the child's baptism. The continuing and especially the everlasting covenant salvation of every child depends upon works the child must perform, that is, upon conditions the child must fulfill. According to the federal vision, some children do perform the conditions and are saved. Other children fail to perform the conditions and, therefore, fall away from Christ, lose their covenant grace, and perish everlastingly.

The conditions of the covenant, according to the federal vision, are faith and obedience—*lifelong* faith and *lifelong* obedience, implying that no one can be sure of persevering in salvation right up to his or her last breath. To the very end, a believer is in real danger of failing to perform the conditions and, therefore, of perishing forever. Always, covenant union with Christ and covenant salvation depend upon the works of the child and, later, upon the man or woman.

Probably, the Reformed Christian is struck by the fact that the federal vision makes lifelong obedience a condition of the covenant. This is openly to teach that salvation is by the good works of the saved sinner, contrary to the declaration of the apostle in Ephesians 2:8–9: "For by grace are ye saved through faith; and that not of yourselves: it is the gift of God: Not of works, lest any man should boast." It is to contradict also the grand statement of the gospel in Romans 9:16: "So then it [salvation] is not of him that willeth, nor of him that runneth [works], but of God that sheweth mercy."

The prophet Jeremiah denies that the new covenant in Christ depends upon the works of the covenant members. He rather teaches that the good works of the members of the new covenant are themselves included in the gracious covenant promise itself and are themselves the fruit of the (irresistible) sanctifying grace of God given to the covenant members and worked in them by the promising God. "I will make a new covenant with the house of Israel, and with the house of Judah...I will put my law in their inward parts, and write it in their hearts" (Jer. 31:31, 33).

According to the gospel of Jeremiah 31, obedience to the law is a benefit of the covenant. According to the federal vision, obedience to the law is a condition of the covenant.

If covenant obedience (the "law") is itself an aspect of covenant salvation, which God freely gives to his covenant people, it cannot be a condition performed by the people upon which the covenant and its salvation depend. But the prophet says that obedience to the law is God's gift to us, sovereignly worked in us by God as no small part of covenant salvation.

From their doctrine that a condition of the covenant is the faithfulness, or obedience, of the children follows the federal vision's heretical doctrine of justification. This is the teaching that justification is not by faith alone, but also by the good works that faith produces. If our good works are a condition of the covenant (as the federal vision teaches), they are also conditions of justification, the chief covenant blessing.

Although our attention is probably concentrated on the teaching of the federal vision that the baptized child's good works are a condition of the covenant (that is, the deed of the child upon which the covenant depends), no less serious (and audacious) is the federal vision's teaching that also faith is a condition of the covenant. For this estimation of faith flies in the face of the teaching of Scripture and the Reformed confessions that faith is the means, or instrument, by which God gives and the elect believer receives righteousness and all salvation. Faith is not a human work that makes one worthy of salvation or upon which one's righteousness and salvation depend. We are not justified *because of faith*, but *by* faith, that is, by means of faith. So it is always in Scripture, for example, Romans 3:28: "Therefore we conclude that a man is justified *by* faith" (emphasis added), that is, through the instrumentality of faith, not *because* we believe, as a work required of us upon which justification depends.

It is bold of the federal vision to promote among Reformed Christians the doctrine that faith is a condition in the face of article 22 of the Belgic Confession:

> Therefore we justly say with Paul [against Rome, the Arminians, and the federal vision], *that we are justified by faith alone*, or *by faith without works*. However, to speak more clearly, we do not mean that faith itself justifies us, for it is only an instrument with which we embrace Christ our Righteousness. But Jesus Christ, imputing to us all his merits, and so many holy works, which he hath done for us and in our stead, is our Righteousness. And faith is an instrument that keeps us in communion with him in all his benefits.[1]

There is still another egregious false doctrine involved in the federal vision's making the faith of the child a covenant condition, that is, a work of the child upon which the continuation of the covenant and everlasting covenant salvation depend. Presenting faith as a condition contradicts the Bible's teaching

---

1 Belgic Confession, Art. 22, in *Creeds of Christendom*, 3:408.

that faith is a gift of God to his elect children. Such is the teaching of Ephesians 2:8–9, quoted above. The Reformed confessions teach authoritatively that faith is a gift of God to the elect.

> Faith is therefore to be considered as the gift of God... because it is in reality conferred, breathed, and infused into him [the elect]...[and] because he who works in man both to will and to do, and indeed all things in all, produces both the will to believe and the act of believing also.[2]

The Canons of Dordt teach that Christ merited faith, among all the other gifts of salvation, for the elect, which he then "confers" upon the elect.[3]

This same creed expressly denies that faith is a condition of the new covenant, as the federal vision now teaches. In the context of the Arminian doctrine of the new covenant, the Canons

> *reject* the errors of those...who teach that Christ by his satisfaction merited neither salvation itself for anyone, nor faith, whereby this satisfaction of Christ unto salvation is effectually appropriated; but that he merited for the Father only the authority or the perfect will to deal again with man, and to prescribe new conditions as he might desire.[4]

Indeed, in so many words the Canons deny that faith, or any other quality or action of men, is a "condition of salvation": "The good pleasure of God is the sole cause of this gracious election; which doth not consist herein that God, foreseeing all possible qualities of human actions, elected certain of these *as a condition of* salvation."[5] Faith is one of the possible qualities and actions of men. It is not a condition of salvation, whether

2   Canons of Dordt, 3–4.14, in ibid., 3:591.

3   Canons of Dordt, 2.8, in ibid., 3:587.

4   Canons of Dordt, 2, Rejection of Errors 3, in *Confessions and Church Order*, 165.

5   Canons of Dordt, 1.10, in *Creeds of Christendom*, 3:583; emphasis added.

salvation in the covenant, on the mission field, or anywhere else. To make faith a condition of salvation in the covenant is nothing but the Arminian heresy condemned at Dordt and now making its appearance in the realm of covenant theology. I repeat in answer to the question: covenant conditions for the federal vision are the child's faith and lifelong obedience.

The men of the federal vision are bold as brass to declare that faith and faithfulness are conditions of the covenant, the performing of which saves a child, and the failure to perform which annuls the covenant with that child. I give a few representative statements by the men of the federal vision.

Conditions were, indeed, attached to the fulfillment of the promises made to Abraham [establishing the covenant with Abraham]...circumcision...faith as a condition...a living and obedient faith...a blameless walk.[6]

God truly brings those people [who eventually fall away and perish everlastingly] into His covenant, into union with Christ. They are "in Him," to use Jesus' words in John 15. They share in His blessings (think of Hebrews 6). They experience His love, but that covenant relationship is *conditional*. It calls for repentance and faith and new obedience. God's choice was not conditional, but life in the covenant is.[7]

The Bible emphatically teaches that man stands under obligation to meet certain conditions if he is to be saved by grace and if he is to be justified in the Final Day...Three obligations stand out clearly as conditions for man's salvation—faith, repentance, and submission to the Lordship of Jesus...[Paul, in Romans 3 and 4] is arguing that circumcision is a specious condition of

6   Shepherd, *Call of Grace*, 13–22.

7   Barach, "Covenant and Election," in *Federal Vision*, 37.

justification while faith is a valid condition. Faith itself,
like works, is a law.[8]

The goal of final salvation remains contingent on
conditions which are yet to be fulfilled. It might be
better to call works a *condition* of final justification.[9]

To be in covenant is to have the treasures of God's mercy
and grace and the love which He has for His own Son
given to you. But the covenant is not *unconditional*.
It requires persevering faithfulness...The covenant is
dependent upon persevering faith.[10]

**Many say these issues in the covenant are simply a matter of
"different terminology." Both sides say it is "all of grace," whether
considered a condition or a necessary means. Is this possible?**

When the theologians, including the ministers, dismiss the
issue of the unconditional or conditional covenant as now
developed by the federal vision as nothing but a difference of
terminology, they deliberately deceive the people (or try to), or
they display appalling ignorance.

The issue is fundamental.

The gospel is at stake.

There are really two aspects to the question. One is the matter
of the confession of salvation by grace by both the federal vision
and its critics: "Both sides say it is 'all of grace.'"

The other is the matter of the term "condition."

I respond to both aspects of the question, beginning with the
matter of the confession of salvation by grace.

The federal vision's doctrine of the conditional covenant
openly and expressly denies the heart of the gospel of salvation
by grace alone, as clearly and authoritatively defined by the

8   P. Andrew Sandlin, "The Gospel of Law and the Law of Gospel: An Assessment
of the Antithetical Gospel-Law Paradigm," in *A Faith That Is Never Alone*, 206–7.

9   Lusk, "Future Justification," in ibid., 318, 342; the emphasis is Lusk's.

10   Wilkins, "Covenant, Baptism, and Salvation," in *Federal Vision*, 64–65; the
emphasis is Wilkins'.

Reformed and Presbyterian creeds: justification by faith alone. With this gospel truth, the federal vision also denies all the doctrines of sovereign grace—the five points of Calvinism—*with regard to salvation in the covenant.*

The dreadful, practical effect of the corruption of the gospel by the men of the federal vision is that they are sending Presbyterian and Reformed men, women, and children (who believe and act on the teaching of the federal vision, as can only be expected in those churches that promote or tolerate the federal vision) into the final judgment *depending for their righteousness before God and their decisive justification upon their own good works.* This is to send these people to their condemnation and eternal damnation, for everyone who appears in God's courtroom of judgment appealing to his or her own works, even in part, as the basis of forgiveness and the verdict of innocence will and must be condemned. This is also to rob these people of all peace in this life and to fill them with terror, for now as they contemplate their final judgment they rest upon their own imperfect works, not upon the perfect work of Christ. "Enter not into judgment with thy servant: for in thy sight shall no man living be justified" (Ps. 143:2). "That no man is justified by the law in the sight of God, it is evident: for, the just shall live by faith" (Gal. 3:11).

That the teaching of justification by works, whether in the final judgment or in one's consciousness in this life, is both damning and distressing is creedal with Reformed Christians.

> Though we do good works, we do not found our salvation upon them [whether in the final judgment, or in this life]; for we can do no work but what is polluted by our flesh, and also punishable; and although we could perform such works, still the remembrance of one sin is sufficient to make God reject them. Thus, then, we should always be in doubt, tossed to and fro without any certainty, and our poor consciences would

be continually vexed if they relied not on the merits of the suffering and death of our Saviour.[11]

The federal vision teaches that the final judgment will be the "decisive" justification of those who will be saved everlastingly, and that that justification will be not by faith alone, but by faith and by the good works of those who then and there will be justified. That is, the federal vision teaches that the decisive justification of sinners is based in part on their own good works (which, of course, the men of the federal vision are quick to add, sinners perform only with the help of grace). This means that the righteousness of sinners that makes them worthy of eternal life is partly their own obedience to the law of God. In the language (but not the doctrine) of Scripture, by the law one can be, must be, and will be justified.

The text mainly appealed to by the advocates and defenders of the federal vision is Romans 2:13: "For not the hearers of the law are just before God, but the doers of the law shall be justified." Ignoring that in the next chapter the apostle will declare that "by the deeds of the law there shall no flesh be justified in his sight: for by the law is the knowledge of sin" (Rom. 3:20), the advocates and defenders of the federal vision explain Romans 2:13 as teaching that in the final judgment justification will actually be the divine verdict upon sinners that takes their deeds of obedience to the law into account in rendering the verdict. Justification will be by doing, not by faith alone.

Norman Shepherd has written:

> [Paul] says in Romans 2:13 that in the Day of Judgment "it is those who obey the law who will be declared righteous." This is...justification by faith, faith that is genuine, faith that works, faith that expresses itself through love. We are not justified by dead faith (faith without works)... We are justified by living and active faith.[12]

---

11   Belgic Confession, Art. 24, in *Creeds of Christendom*, 3:412.

12   Shepherd, "Faith and Faithfulness," in *A Faith That Is Never Alone*, 66.

Rich Lusk is bold. "[Our good] works [are] a *condition* of final justification." "The works that justify at the last day are the works that flow out of a faith that has already received initial acceptance." "Final justification is by faith and works together." "In the final installment of our justification, there is a very real sense in which works will be the *decisive* factor."[13] Richard Gaffin Jr. agrees that Romans 2:13 (which has become the critical text in the controversy of Reformed orthodoxy with the heresy of the federal vision regarding justification, as it was an important text in the conflict of the Reformation with Rome) teaches actual justification in the final judgment by faith and by the sinner's own doing. "The broader biblical context suggests that the positive outcome in view in Romans 2:5ff., at least in verses 5–11, *if not verses 12–13 as well*, is best seen as describing what will be true of Christians at the final judgment."[14]

All these loudly proclaim that salvation is by grace, as Rome has ever also loudly proclaimed that salvation is by grace, especially when its doctrine of salvation by works is attacked.

But to deny that justification is by faith alone, apart from all the works of the elect sinner, including the good works he performs by the grace of the Spirit (or to say it differently, by virtue of his union with Christ), is to deny salvation by grace.

One truly confesses salvation by grace when his confession includes that justification is by faith alone, apart from any and all good works of the sinner himself, whether performed with or without the help of grace.

One truly confesses salvation by grace when his confession adds the word "alone": "by grace *alone*."

And one truly confesses salvation by grace *alone* when his confession includes that this grace is sovereign and particular.

The federal vision is not introducing new heresies into the Reformed churches. It is not even merely resurrecting old heresies. The federal vision is developing false doctrines

13 Lusk, "Future Justification" in ibid., 342–43, 354, 318; the emphasis is Lusk's.

14 Gaffin, *By Faith, Not By Sight*, 97; emphasis added.

that have taken root in Reformed and Presbyterian churches, indeed, false doctrines that many of the conservative Reformed and Presbyterian churches have vigorously defended, *and still do defend*, against the criticism of them by the Protestant Reformed Churches. By the federal vision, God is now putting conservative Reformed and Presbyterian churches to the test concerning the truth of their avowed confession of "grace alone." He is exposing the false doctrine concerning grace either officially adopted by some of them or commonly taught in others. He calls them to reexamine this false doctrine and repudiate it. If they refuse to do so, they knowingly concede the logical and inevitable development of this false doctrine in the theology of the federal vision.

I refer to the doctrine that in the preaching of the gospel God is gracious to all men without exception, at least to all those who hear the preaching of the gospel, both those who are saved by the gospel and those who go lost. This is the doctrine of a grace of God *that is wider in extent than election*. This is the doctrine of a (saving) grace of God that is *resistible*.

To a man the proponents of the federal vision would say, and do say, vehemently, that salvation is by grace alone. But their saving grace—in the covenant—is a grace of God in Christ that is shown to, and bestowed upon, all the baptized infants alike. It is a grace that is wider than the eternal decree of election. It is, therefore, a grace that fails to save some to whom it is shown and upon whom it is bestowed. It is a (saving) grace that is resistible. This necessarily implies that for its efficacy, that is, for the actual, everlasting salvation of those to whom it is given, grace depends upon an act, decision, deeds, or worthiness (or all of these) of the sinner himself.

This is the denial of salvation by grace alone, no matter how loudly and vehemently the theologians and ministers shout, "Salvation is by grace alone."

Universal grace that fails to save some is resistible grace, and resistible grace means that salvation, in the final analysis and at the decisive point, depends upon and is effected by sinful man.

At bottom, the heresy of Arminianism, as exposed and condemned by the Synod of Dordt, was (and still is) the doctrine of universal, resistible grace.

The only effective repudiation of Arminianism was (and is) the Canons' teaching that the (saving) grace of God is particular (having its source and determination in the eternal decree of election, accompanied by an equally eternal reprobation that withholds grace from all the nonelect). The only effective repudiation of Arminianism was (and is) the Canons' teaching that the (saving) grace of God is sovereign, or irresistibly almighty (effectually accomplishing the full salvation of everyone to whom this grace is shown and upon whom it is bestowed, failing to save none to whom God directs his grace).

Denying the particularity and sovereignty of grace—in the covenant—the federal vision denies salvation by grace alone. It teaches salvation by the will and works of the baptized babies.

In order to refute the federal vision, the Reformed churches must confess that the grace by which alone we are saved *is particular and irresistible*. And this will mean for many of them that they must confess their own sin of teaching that the grace of God in Christ in the gospel is a well-meant offer to all hearers, that is, that the gospel is God's (saving) grace toward all hearers alike, those who finally go lost as well as those who finally are saved.

How popular this doctrine is even in conservative churches that have not officially or semi-officially adopted the teaching of universal, resistible grace in the preaching, the common explanation of John 3:16 shows. How many preachers in conservative Reformed churches do not explain John 3:16 as teaching that the love of God that gave his only begotten Son is universal, that is, for all humans without exception, and that this love gave the Son for all humans without exception. How many do not also explain the text in such a way as to make faith the condition upon which the efficacy of the love of God depends. This is the teaching of universal, resistible grace. There is no essential difference between it and the doctrine of the federal vision. The only differences are that the federal vision emphasizes the love of God toward all the baptized babies of believers and that the federal vision more boldly and explicitly states that the continuation and efficacy of this love of God in Christ depend upon acts that the babies must perform.

In light of the federal vision, many conservative Reformed churches and multitudes of conservative Reformed ministers must repudiate their own doctrine of universal, resistible grace in the preaching of the gospel.

Salvation is not by grace alone, if the grace that saves is not sovereign and particular.

The second aspect of the question concerns the term "condition": "condition or necessary means."

The question is this: Is there not a use of the term "condition" in Reformed covenant doctrine that is proper—a use that does not necessarily deny salvation by (sovereign, particular) grace in the covenant, specifically, the salvation of baptized, covenant infants? And does not this proper use of condition justify the conditional covenant doctrine of the men of the federal vision?

In the late 1940s and early 1950s those Protestant Reformed ministers who caused schism in the denomination by introducing the conditional covenant doctrine of the Reformed Churches in the Netherlands (liberated), the doctrine of the covenant now being developed by the federal vision, defended their position by speaking of "Reformed conditions." Is there such a thing?

In the past some orthodox Reformed theologians and, indeed, the Westminster standards have spoken of a condition of the covenant in such a sense as did not compromise the truth of salvation by grace alone. The seventeenth-century Swiss theologian and successor at Geneva of John Calvin and Theodore Beza, Francis Turretin, was one of these theologians. The Westminster Larger Catechism speaks of the "condition" of the covenant:

How is the grace of God manifested in the second covenant?

The grace of God is manifested in the second covenant, in that he freely provideth and offereth to sinners a Mediator, and life and salvation by him; and requiring faith as the condition to interest them in him, promiseth and giveth his Holy Spirit to all his elect, to work in them that faith, with all other saving graces; and to enable them unto all holy obedience, as the evidence of the truth of their faith and thankfulness to God, and as the way which he hath appointed them to salvation.[15]

This use of "condition" refers to faith as the necessary means or way by which God realizes his covenant with, and bestows covenant salvation upon, his elect and the way in which the elect receive and enjoy salvation. The Westminster Catechism speaks of faith as "the condition *to interest them in him.*"

This use of "condition" recognizes, indeed expressly states, that God establishes his covenant with Christ and with the elect in him. Immediately preceding Westminster's description of faith as the condition is the Catechism's declaration that the covenant of grace "was made with Christ as the second Adam, and in him with all the elect as his seed"[16]

This use of "condition" affirms that the covenant promise is made only to the elect and includes that God will surely give them faith: "promiseth and giveth his Holy Spirit to all his elect, to work in them that faith."

This use of "condition" declares in the same breath that faith is the gift of God to the elect: "to work in them that faith."

Radically different is the use of "condition" with reference to faith by the federal vision and by the conditional covenant doctrine that the federal vision is busy developing. First, the federal vision does not regard faith as *the* condition, but as one of many conditions, the others being good works, repentance, faithfulness, and more. This already makes plain that the federal vision by "condition" is not describing faith as the (sole) means of covenant salvation.

Second, the federal vision calls faith a condition in connection with its doctrine that God makes his covenant of grace with

15 Westminster Larger Catechism, Q&A 32, in *Confession of Faith and Subordinate Standards*, 57.

16 Westminster Larger Catechism, A. 31, in ibid., 57.

all the baptized babies alike, not with the elect alone. This marks the fundamental difference between a use of "condition" that does not contradict grace and the use of "condition" that does contradict grace. To teach that faith is the condition of a gracious covenant established with many more than the elect is to teach that faith is *a work of the children upon which the covenant depends* and *by which some distinguish themselves from others*.

Third, the federal vision teaches that faith is a condition of the fulfillment of God's gracious covenant promise, made in grace to all the baptized babies alike. This means that faith is *a work of the children that makes the promise effectual* in their case and *a work of the children upon which the promise of God depends*.

Fourth, in teaching that the gracious covenant promise is made to all the baptized children alike, the federal vision necessarily denies that faith is part of the promise. If faith itself is part of the promise, if God in addressing the promise to children includes faith, that is, if God promises, "I will be your God, I will save you, I will give you faith," either the promise results in the faith and salvation of all the baptized babies of believers, or God is a liar. But the federal vision denies that all the children to whom God makes the covenant promise are saved; many go lost. Neither does the federal vision like to call God a liar. The explanation is that in the theology of the federal vision the covenant promise does not include faith. Therefore, what the federal vision means by teaching that faith is a condition is that faith is *a work of the children themselves (whether with or without the help of grace makes no difference) upon which the promise, covenant, and covenant salvation depend*.

All the emphasis of the federal vision regarding faith is upon its being a requirement and responsibility of the baptized children. If any of the men of the federal vision ever say that faith is the gracious gift of God to a child, it is a rarity and an inconsistency. According to the federal vision, God graciously establishes the covenant with all alike; God graciously makes the promise to all alike; God even graciously unites all alike to

Christ and begins to give the blessings of the covenant to all alike. Faith is a demand upon the child, and upon the child's compliance with this demand everything depends. Faith is condition *in this sense.*

Subtle as he is in teaching that faith is a condition in the sense that it is purely a work of man upon which God's grace depends for its saving effect, Norman Shepherd could not restrain himself from making this plain. "These [grace and faith] are the two parts of the covenant: grace and faith, promise and obligation. Grace is not without conditions."[17] For Shepherd, faith is not part of grace, as it is in Romans 4:16, Ephesians 2:8, and the third and fourth heads of the Canons. Nor is it part of the promise, as is the teaching of the Westminster Larger Catechism, question and answer 32. But it is an entirely separate element of the covenant. Faith is not God's grace, neither is it included in God's gracious promise. Rather, it is man's obligation, man's work, man's effort, man's willing and running. And upon this second element, which is not part of grace, does the grace of God depend from beginning to end.

What Shepherd teaches craftily, the other men of the federal vision teach openly, as I have demonstrated in earlier chapters: Faith is a condition in the sense that the continuation of the covenant; the continued enjoyment of covenant blessings; justification, especially in the final judgment; and eternal life depend upon this act of the baptized children. And by failing to perform the condition of the covenant a child resists grace, frustrates the gracious promise, separates himself from Christ, loses the blessings of the covenant (including justification), and falls out of and away from covenant salvation.

The federal vision's use of "condition" to describe faith is radically different from the use of "condition" by orthodox theologians in the past and by the Westminster standards. The federal vision does not mean by condition the necessary means by which God certainly realizes his covenant with the elect. The federal vision does not refer to faith as the necessary means

17 Shepherd, *Call of Grace,* 63.

of covenant salvation that God promises to the elect in Christ, and to them alone, and that he works in them by his sovereign Holy Spirit. Not at all! The federal vision and the conditional covenant doctrine that the federal vision is developing mean by condition a work of the child upon which the covenant and its salvation depend and a work of some children by which they distinguish themselves from others, who are as much the objects of the gracious promise and as much the recipients of covenant grace as themselves.

This use of "condition" is the overthrow of the gospel of salvation by grace alone—*with regard to the covenant.*

I conclude my answer by briefly noting the following.

First, regarding the use of "condition" by such orthodox theologians as Francis Turretin, he remarked:

[If the word "condition" has the sense of a] meritorious and impulsive cause and for a natural condition [which is the proper sense of the word], the covenant of grace is rightly denied to be conditioned. It is wholly gratuitous, depending upon the sole good will...of God and upon no merit of man. Nor can the right to life be founded upon any action of ours, but on the righteousness of Christ alone...The covenant does not rest upon a condition in us, but upon the mere grace of God and his inviolable faithfulness and the infinite merit of Christ."[18]

According to Turretin, that the covenant is unconditional must be said "first."[19] (It is significant that the men of the federal vision do not speak of the covenant's being unconditional first, second, or last. According to them, the covenant is not unconditional whatsoever.)

By allowing that the covenant may also, second, be said to be conditional, Turretin meant only that faith is the instrument, or means, of the receiving and enjoying of the covenant: "[The

18   Francis Turretin, *Institutes of Elenctic Theology*, vol. 2, ed. James T. Dennison Jr., trans. George Musgrave Giger, (Phillipsburg, NJ: P&R, 1994), 185–86.

19   Turretin, ibid., 185.

evangelical condition of the covenant, namely, faith] may only be called an instrument by which the thing promised is apprehended (Acts 26:18; Rom. 5:17) and without which it cannot be obtained (Heb. 11:6)"[20]

Herman Bavinck agreed. "In the covenant of grace, that is, in the gospel, which is the proclamation of the covenant of grace, there are actually no demands and no conditions. For God supplies what he demands. Christ has accomplished everything... and the Holy Spirit therefore applies them." Bavinck only allows that the administration of the covenant assumes a "conditional *form*."[21] This analysis of the covenant as unconditional by the Dutch theologian occurs in the context of Bavinck's insistence that election governs the covenant, a truth that is abhorrent to the federal vision, as to the covenant doctrine that the federal vision is developing.

Second, the Bible never describes faith as a condition, that is, as the activity of the sinner upon which justification and salvation depend. It always describes faith as the means or source—source inasmuch as faith is union with Christ. Elect sinners, whether in the covenant or on the mission field, are saved not on account of faith, but by means of faith. "By grace are ye saved *through* faith" (Eph. 2:8, emphasis added). "We have believed in Jesus Christ, that we might be justified *by* the faith of Christ" (Gal. 2:16, emphasis added).

Third, the three forms of unity not only never call faith a condition, but also explicitly repudiate viewing faith as a condition. "This election was not founded upon foreseen faith... as the prerequisite, cause, or condition on which it depended; but men are chosen to faith and to the obedience of faith."[22] The doctrine that faith is a condition, particularly a condition of the new covenant, was the teaching of the Arminians. Surely, the men of the federal vision know this.

---

20   Turretin, ibid., 186.

21   Bavinck, *Reformed Dogmatics*, 3:230; emphasis added.

22   Canons of Dordt, 1.9, in *Creeds of Christendom*, 3:583.

Surely, the purported critics of the federal vision know this also. Why then do these critics never criticize the conditional covenant doctrine of the men of the federal vision? Why do they never even so much as acknowledge that there is today, and has always been, in the Reformed churches a doctrine of an unconditional covenant, with powerful backing in the Reformed confessions? Why do they not consider that they are called by God on the occasion of the heresy of the federal vision to reconsider the great issue of the conditionality or unconditionality of the covenant—an issue that has troubled the Reformed churches down the ages?

Fourth, in the controversy of the Protestant Reformed Churches in the early 1950s over the very issue that now confronts the entire Reformed community in the theology of the federal vision—the doctrine of the covenant of grace, unconditional or conditional?—Herman Hoeksema made plain exactly what the Protestant Reformed Churches were rejecting when they repudiated the Schilderian and liberated doctrine of a conditional covenant—the root of the federal vision. Hoeksema noted, shrewdly, that although his opponents claimed to be defending "conditions in the Reformed sense," none of them gave "a clear-cut definition of such conditions." He challenged them: "Let someone present such a definition, and then let us test it. No one has ever made an attempt at this, not even Dr. Schilder."[23]

Hoeksema himself then defined "condition" as the word actually functions in the liberated doctrine of the covenant: "a prerequisite which someone must fulfill in order to receive something from someone else." He added: "Apply that definition of conditions to the work of salvation, and you have pure Arminianism."[24]

In this proper sense of the word "condition," the Protestant Reformed Churches rejected the doctrine of a conditional covenant in 1951–53.

23 Herman Hoeksema, "The Synod of 1951," *Standard Bearer* 28, no. 8 (January 15, 1952): 173.

24 Hoeksema, ibid.

The Protestant Reformed Churches were not denying that faith is the necessary means of salvation. In the Declaration of Principles that rejects the doctrine of a conditional covenant, it is affirmed that "the preaching comes to all; and that God seriously commands to faith and repentance; and that to all those who come and believe He promises life and peace."[25] The teaching of faith as a condition *in the sense of a prerequisite that the sinner must fulfill in order to make a general, gracious promise effectual in his own case,* or *in the sense of a work of the sinful child upon which the continuation and fulfillment of the covenant depend,* is a denial of salvation by grace alone.

Having recognized that orthodox Reformed theologians in the past used "condition" in such a sense (necessary means of salvation) as did not compromise the gospel of salvation by grace alone, I add that even then the use of "condition" was not only an improper use of it, but also theologically risky. It lay open to misunderstanding and misuse, as though salvation depended upon something the sinner must do.

The use of the word "condition" by heretics, especially the Arminians, to promote their doctrines of salvation by the will and working of man ought to move contemporary theologians who are zealous on behalf of the gospel of grace to purge "condition" from their covenant vocabulary altogether. Bavinck, in the context of the passage already cited, makes this very point. "In the beginning Reformed theologians spoke freely of 'the conditions' of the covenant. But after the nature of the covenant of grace had been more carefully considered and had to be defended against Catholics, Lutherans, and Remonstrants [Arminians], many of them took exception to the term and avoided it."[26]

It is intriguing that Bavinck praised those who "took exception to the term ['conditions'] and avoided it" in their

25 Declaration of Principles of the Protestant Reformed Churches, in *Confessions and Church Order*, 426.

26 Bavinck, *Reformed Dogmatics*, 3:229.

doctrine of the covenant, as champions of grace against the advocates of man's will and works. Contemporary Reformed theologians, in contrast, almost to a man, purported critics of the federal vision as well as the men of the federal vision, can only vilify those Reformed theologians who avoid the term in the interests of rejecting the covenant doctrine of Rome and of the Arminians.

Reformed theologians and churches ought to take exception to the term "condition" because of the "nature of the covenant of grace" and in order to defend grace against its enemies. All the more ought the Reformed churches to look askance at the term "condition" when they take note of a deplorable development of the doctrine of the covenant over past centuries in some Reformed and Presbyterian traditions. This is a view of the covenant in every phase of its revelation as virtually a bargain.

Does the covenant originate in eternity with God? The origin is conceived as a bargain between Father and Son, bristling with conditions.

Was the relation of Adam with God a covenant? This too must have been a bargain between the creator and his creature, with the interdependent conditions of a business deal.

So also the covenant of grace is viewed as a contract, a conditional relationship: God will do such and such if man will do this and that. And God will not do this and that, if man declines to do such and such.

At the heart of this cold, unattractive covenant conception, in which grace—the sheer, glorious, particular, sovereign grace of God in Jesus Christ—gets buried, lurks the word "condition" in its proper sense: that upon which something (divine grace) or someone (God himself) depends.

May God grant that the federal vision serves the healthy purpose of ridding the Reformed churches of this unbiblical conception of the covenant once and for all! And with it the term "condition"! That is, may God grant that this heresy too serves the purifying and developing of the church's knowledge and confession of the truth!

Whatever may be the outcome in the controversy of Reformed orthodoxy with the federal vision, at stake is the gospel of grace.

What about the if/then statements in the Bible, for example, Deuteronomy 7:12–13 and Deuteronomy 11:13–17? These statements seem conditional. Do the men of the federal vision latch on to these? How are these statements to be explained?

The men of the federal vision do indeed "latch on" to these statements, with both hands—and with heart, mind, soul, and strength. So did Pelagius, Desiderius Erasmus, Albertus Pighius, Jacob Arminius, and Simon Episcopius. From these statements, the federal vision constructs a conditional gospel, that is, a gospel of God's dependency upon sinners in salvation. So did Pelagius, Erasmus, Pighius, Arminius, and Episcopius.

The Reformed churches have officially rejected the explanation of these if/then statements as teaching a conditional gospel. They have rejected this explanation of these statements in the Canons of Dordt. The Canons of Dordt explain the if/then statements in Scripture, as well as all the rest of Scripture, as teaching an unconditional gospel, that is, a gospel that proclaims that from beginning to end the salvation of sinners depends upon God, upon God only, and not at all, in any sense whatever, upon sinners.

Head one confesses that "election is the fountain of every saving good" and that this election "was not founded upon foreseen faith, and the obedience of faith, holiness, or any other good quality or disposition in man, as the prerequisite, cause, or condition on which it depended."[27] This all by itself settles the matter. If election is the source of all salvation, *including salvation in the covenant*, and if election is unconditional, all of salvation is unconditional, *including salvation in the covenant*. That is, salvation depends solely upon God.

But in order to guard against the explanation of the if/then statements by Pelagius, Erasmus, Pighius, Arminius, and the men of the federal vision, the Holy Spirit had the fathers of

27 Canons of Dordt, 1.9, in *Creeds of Christendom*, 3:583.

Dordt add that also the atonement of Christ is unconditional. It is unconditional both with regard to what the death of Christ accomplished then and there and with regard to its application to the soul of the elect child of God. That Christ died the redeeming death of the cross was due solely to "the sovereign counsel and most gracious will and purpose of God the Father." The application of this death in all its redemptive benefit *does not depend upon the sinner*, for "faith…[and] all the other saving gifts," Christ "*purchased* for [the elect] by his death." Further, rather than that faith and holiness of life are conditions upon which the application of the cross depends, Christ "*confer[s]…faith [and]…all the other saving gifts*" upon the elect.[28]

The Canons establish in the third and fourth heads of doctrine that the regeneration, justification, and sanctification of the elect sinner are unconditional, that is, that the meaning of the if/then statements in the Bible is not what the men of the federal vision teach. Prior to union with Christ and regeneration, every sinner (whether pagan adult on the mission field or infant of godly parents) is by nature "dead in sin, and in bondage thereto," incapable, therefore, of performing any condition unto salvation.[29]

The continuation of the salvation of a regenerated man or woman is also unconditional, according to the Canons. The Canons affirm that faith is the "gift of God," not only as a power in the elect sinner, but also as the continual activity of believing: "[God] produces both the will to believe and the act of believing also."[30] Faith is not a condition performed by the sinner, but is the gift of God.

Also with regard to the relation between grace and faith in the regenerated and converted child of God, this relation is not that grace—*continued* grace—is dependent upon, that is, conditioned by, the sinner's believing and repenting. Rather,

---

28   Canons of Dordt, 2.8, in ibid., 3:587; emphasis added.

29   Canons of Dordt, 3–4.1–3, in ibid., 3:587–88.

30   Canons of Dordt, 3–4.14, in ibid., 3:591.

the converted sinner is "rightly said to believe and repent, *by virtue of that grace received.*"[31] That is, our believing and our repenting *are dependent upon the grace of God.*

The men of the federal vision are especially prone to explain the if/then statements of Scripture as teaching that the perseverance of saved sinners unto final glory depends upon conditions they must perform. They enthusiastically proclaim the terrifying implication, namely, the possibility that some saved sinners lose their salvation and perish eternally. The Canons condemn this doctrine—this explanation of the if/then statements of Scripture—in the fifth head of doctrine. Perseverance "in a state of grace" unto life everlasting is not a condition performed by the sinner. Rather, "God is faithful, who having conferred grace, mercifully confirms and powerfully preserves them [all who have been united to Christ and converted] therein, even to the end."[32] It is not due to anything whatever in those who persevere in grace and salvation that they do thus persevere. Rather, "it is...of God's free mercy, that they do not totally fall from faith and grace."[33]

The word for this unconditional salvation, from eternal election to everlasting glory, is *grace.*

The Canons' explanation of the if/then statements in the Bible, as also of all the statements of the Bible, that is, of the one, unified message of salvation in Scripture, is of binding authority for all who profess to be Reformed, including the men of the federal vision. If the men of the federal vision judge the Canons to be mistaken in their explanation of the if/then statements in the Bible, they must formally object. Honesty requires that they publicly inform the Reformed people whom they seek to instruct that they differ from the Canons regarding the if/then statements in the Bible.

The creeds *settle issues.* They determine what is biblical and Reformed, *once and for all.* Reformed churches and people do

31 Canons of Dordt, 3–4.12, in ibid., 3:590; emphasis added.

32 Canons of Dordt, 5.3, in ibid., 3:593.

33 Canons of Dordt, 5.8, in ibid., 3:594.

not have to be forever reinventing the wheel. Reformed churches and people are not in such a position and in such a frame of mind as allows Pelagianism and Arminianism to come up again and again in new forms in their midst as legitimate subjects of fresh discussion and debate. They are *creedally* Reformed.

To the conditional theology of the federal vision, the Reformed and Presbyterian churches have said no, decisively. (The Westminster standards teach the same unconditional gospel as the Canons.)

With regard to the if/then statements in Deuteronomy 7:12–13 and Deuteronomy 11:13–17, these statements do not merely seem to be conditional. They *are* conditional statements—*grammatically*. But grammatically conditional statements in the Bible do not teach a *conditional gospel*, any more than symbolic texts teach a symbolic gospel.

Every if/then statement in the Bible must be explained in the light of its context. Not all have the same meaning. The texts in Deuteronomy and similar texts in the Old Testament taught the true Israel of God in the Old Testament to look to the coming Messiah for their salvation, inasmuch as they could not, and did not, perform the "if." This is the explanation of the if/then texts, as well as all the law of the Old Testament, by Galatians 3:24: "The law was our schoolmaster to bring us unto Christ, that we might be justified by faith." No Israelite ever did, or *could*, perform the "if" part of the if/then statements. Jesus Christ would "hearken to these judgments, and keep, and do them"—*perfectly*—in the stead of the true Israel of God and thus confirm the covenant with Israel/church.

In addition, the if/then statements in the Old Testament called the believing Israelite, who was freely justified by faith in the coming Messiah, to thankful obedience to God's commandments as the way in which he would continue to receive and enjoy God's covenant salvation. These statements called the godly to their part in the covenant, establishing their covenantal responsibility. In response, the godly believed,

repented, and obeyed—gladly, willingly, heartily, faithfully—
"by virtue of...grace received."[34]
At the same time, these if/then statements maintained the
responsibility of the reprobate ungodly in Israel. The statements
set before them the way of life and the way of death and
commanded them, seriously, to choose life. For their refusal to
walk in the ways of the covenant, they were to blame.

This explanation of the if/then statements in Scripture is
Reformed orthodoxy, as determined by the creeds and in harmony with the gospel of grace.

**You say that God is not "dependent" on the sinner. The men
of the federal vision would respond that God has chosen to
require faith of the sinner. It is God's choosing. What would
be your answer?**

The question is this, really: Cannot God be dependent upon
the sinner, as the federal vision indeed teaches, *by virtue of
his own act of making himself dependent on the sinner, by
requiring faith of him?*

The Reformed faith, which the men of the federal vision
profess to teach, confesses that God is independent not only of
sinners, but also of everything.

> God hath all life, glory, goodness, blessedness, in
> and of himself; *and is alone in and unto himself all-
> sufficient*, not standing in need of any creatures which
> he hath made, nor deriving any glory from them,
> but only manifesting his own glory in, by, unto, and
> upon them: *he is the alone fountain of all being, of
> whom, through whom, and to whom are all things*;
> and *hath most sovereign dominion over them, to do
> by them, for them, or upon them whatsoever himself
> pleaseth*. In his sight all things are open and manifest;
> *his knowledge is infinite, infallible, and independent
> upon the creature; so as nothing is to him contingent
> or uncertain*...To him is due from angels and men, and

34   Canons of Dordt, 3–4.12, in ibid., 3:590; emphasis added.

every other creature, whatsoever worship, service, or obedience, he is pleased to require of them.[35]

This is God.

God can no more willingly give up his independency and remain God than he can voluntarily give up his almightiness or holiness and still be God. The teaching that God is dependent upon the sinner, which is the doctrine of the federal vision, is an open attack on the Godhead of God. This is the seriousness of the controversy of Reformed orthodoxy with the federal vision.

And then to teach that God's dependency is his dependence on sinners for their salvation adds, if possible, to the wickedness of the heresy. This teaching has God giving the glory of his greatest work—salvation—to the sinful creature. Less reprehensible would be making God dependent on creatures for their creation or for their continued existence.

The appeal to the requirement of faith in support of God's purported stripping of himself of his independency, that is, his all-sufficiency and his noncontingency, in salvation is, well... perverse. First, faith is dependence on God—utter dependency upon God in Jesus Christ for salvation. This is what God requires: complete dependency upon him. To turn the truth of faith upside down, so that it now becomes God's dependency upon the sinner, is perverse.

Second, the faith that God requires *he also gives.*

Faith is therefore to be considered as the gift of God, not on account of its being offered by God to man, to be accepted or rejected at his pleasure, but because it is in reality conferred, breathed, and infused into him; nor even because God bestows the power or ability to believe, and then expects that man should, by the exercise of his own free will, consent to the terms of salvation, and actually believe in Christ; but because he who works in man both to will and to do, and indeed

---

all things in all, produces both the will to believe and the act of believing also.[36]

We sinners depend upon God in believing. We sinners depend upon God for our believing. In faith and for faith, we are as dependent upon God as we are for our next breath.

You state that the conditionality of the covenant is the "root" of the problem of the federal vision. Would it not be more correct to state that the denial of God's sovereignty is the root of the problem?

I regard these two truths—the sovereignty of God and the unconditionality of the covenant—as intimately related. The unconditionality of the covenant is the expression and benefit of the sovereignty of the grace of God. The sovereignty of the covenant grace of God is its effectual, invincible, irresistible power—the almighty power of God himself—accomplishing in every case the purpose, or desire, of God to establish, maintain, and perfect his covenant relation with his elect in Jesus Christ. The sovereignty of the grace of God in Jesus Christ accounts for the unconditionality of the covenant. "For with God nothing shall be impossible" (Luke 1:37).

The doctrine of a conditional covenant—a covenant that can be broken by men with whom God has graciously established the covenant (the teaching of the federal vision)—is a denial of the sovereignty of God. In principle, the doctrine of a conditional covenant is the affirmation of the sovereignty of the sinner in (covenant) salvation.

I agree, therefore, that when the root of the heresy of the federal vision—the conditional covenant—is traced down to its deepest tendril, that tendril will be discovered to be the denial of the sovereignty of God, that is, the denial that God is God.

36 Canons of Dordt, 3–4.14, in ibid., 3:591.

How do the federal vision people respond when we accuse them of believing that their faith is a condition?

The men of the federal vision respond by saying, "Exactly so! This is what we teach: Faith is a condition of the covenant. But so also is a life of good works a condition upon which the covenant depends."

THE FEDERAL VISION AND SCRIPTURE

The phrase "covenant of grace" is not in Scripture. Could you give four or five passages of Scripture showing this covenant plainly?

Although the phrase "covenant of grace" does not occur in Scripture, it is found in the Reformed creeds, which by the phrase rightly express the teaching of Scripture. These creeds, of course, are authoritative for Reformed men and women.

The Canons of Dordt speak of the "new covenant of grace" in the rejection of errors section of the second head of doctrine, articles 2 and 4. Canons 2, Rejection of Errors 2 reads:

> The Synod *rejects* the errors of those...who teach that it was not the purpose of the death of Christ that He should confirm the new covenant of grace through His blood, but only that He should acquire for the Father the mere right to establish with man such a covenant as He might please, whether of grace or of works.[1]

That the Canons call the covenant a "covenant of grace" in this section is significant regarding the present controversy of Reformed orthodoxy with the federal vision. In this section the Canons condemn the Arminian teaching that on the basis of the cross God makes the covenant with many more humans than only the elect, *conditionally*. Essentially, this is the error of the federal vision.

---

1 Canons of Dordt, 2, Rejection of Errors 2, in *Confessions and Church Order*, 164.

The Reformed baptism form states that "when we are baptized in the name of the Father, God the Father witnesseth and sealeth unto us, that he doth make an eternal covenant of grace with us."[2]

The Reformed Lord's supper form teaches that by his death Christ "confirmed…the new and eternal testament, that covenant of grace and reconciliation."[3]

This confessional testimony is based on, and expresses the truth of, such passages of Scripture as the following.

Genesis 17:7 teaches the establishment of the covenant with Abraham and his seed (that is, with Christ, according to Galatians 3:16) out of the free favor of God, and the free favor of God only.

Psalm 89:28–37 teaches the faithful maintenance of the covenant with Christ and those who are his by election in the free favor and by the irresistible saving power of God, and the free favor and irresistible power of God only.

Jeremiah 31:31–34 teaches the working of new obedience, that is, our covenant faithfulness and our part in the covenant, in the members of the covenant by the sovereign, saving power of God, and the sovereign power of God only.

Luke 1:67–75 teaches the establishment, maintenance, and perfection of the covenant as the work of God in the incarnation and ministry of Jesus Christ in amazing favor to guilty and depraved sinners, and the work of God in amazing favor only.

Hebrews 8–10 teaches the new covenant coming to all who enjoy it by faith, as that graciously willed to them by God (a testament) and as that obtained for them and made effectual with them by the death of Jesus Christ and by the will of God and on the basis of the death of Christ only.

The description "covenant of grace" means something. "Covenant of grace" may not become an empty, indeed deceiving, cliché in Reformed circles. Arminian preachers also speak of a

2 Form for the Administration of Baptism, in ibid., 258.
3 Form for the Administration of the Lord's Supper, in ibid., 270.

"covenant of grace"—often and loudly. In fact, however, they teach a "covenant of the will and works of man."

"Covenant of grace" means that the covenant of God in Christ with men, women, and children is grace—pure grace, grace only, grace from beginning to end. It means that the covenant is established, maintained, and perfected with believers and their children out of the sovereign, free favor of God, by the irresistible, saving power of God (the Spirit of Christ), and on the basis of the atoning death of Jesus Christ.

"Covenant of grace" means, negatively, that the covenant does not depend, whatsoever, in any respect, upon man.

"Covenant of grace" means, negatively, that the covenant is not established, is not maintained, and is not perfected on the basis of or by the power of the will, works, and worthiness of those with whom the covenant is established.

That is, "covenant of grace" means that the covenant is not conditional.

The "covenant of grace" is not the covenant of the federal vision.

How do the proponents of the federal vision then defend themselves against Romans 9?

Romans 9 exposes the false doctrine that is the root of the federal vision: the denial that God's eternal predestination governs the covenant with believers and their children.

The federal vision teaches that God makes his gracious covenant promise to all the children of believers alike; graciously makes his covenant with all the children alike (at their baptism); and unites them all alike to Christ, so that all begin to receive the new life of Christ and the covenant blessings, including justification. All the children alike are the objects of God's gracious attitude (his desire to save them), and all alike actually receive covenant grace in their hearts. However, whether a child remains in the covenant, continues to enjoy the blessings of salvation, and is saved everlastingly depend upon his performing the conditions of the covenant.

The federal vision teaches that all the children alike are elect *in the sense that election has in Ephesians 1:4 and in*

2 Thessalonians 2:13 and, therefore, virtually everywhere in the Bible. Election for the federal vision is a choice God makes in time and history. God's election is changeable. I have already quoted Douglas Wilson as affirming that God's election of people often changes into reprobation, depending on whether the people perform the conditions. Election unto covenant grace and (temporary) covenant salvation is conditional for the federal vision.

Romans 9 is the refutation of this fundamental teaching of the federal vision.

Romans 9 teaches that God's covenant promise to the children of Abraham; his making of his covenant with the children of Abraham; his blessing of the children of Abraham with the blessings of the covenant, including justification; and his saving of the children of Abraham had their source in God's eternal election and were governed by the eternal decree. The word of covenant promise, the covenant itself, covenant blessings, and covenant salvation were for only some of Abraham's children, not for all of them.

The apostle is explaining in Romans 9 why the unbelief and perishing of so many of Abraham's physical offspring are not evidence that the "word of God" has failed: "Not as though the word of God hath taken none effect" (v. 6). The "word of God" is the covenant promise to Abraham, "I will be the God of your seed." The apostle's explanation is that not all the physical offspring of Abraham were "Israel" (v. 6). Many were only "of Israel," that is, merely connected outwardly to the nation. Only some of Abraham's offspring were (true) "Israel."

The covenant promise of God was only for those children of Abraham who were "Israel." And the word of promise saved all of them.

The question is: What explains the difference between the two kinds of children of Abraham: those children who were truly "Israel" and those children who were merely "of Israel"?

The apostle's answer is: the eternal election of some, and some only, unto (covenant) salvation. Only some of Abraham's children were "children of the promise," who were counted by

God for the seed of Abraham when he promised to be the God of Abraham's seed (v. 8). And it was God's eternal election that set them apart, distinguished them from the other children, and made them the objects of God's covenant grace. The apostle proves this from a clear instance in the Old Testament: God's eternal election of Jacob unto covenant grace and salvation in distinction from his twin brother, Esau, whom God hated and reprobated from eternity (vv. 10–13: "that the purpose of God according to election might stand," v. 11).

Romans 9 addresses, and settles, the fundamental issue at stake in the controversy raised by the federal vision. God's eternal election is the source of the covenant, of covenant grace, of covenant blessings, and of covenant salvation.

God's election governs the covenant.

The apostle finally quotes God himself to establish this truth, namely, that election governs the covenant. In Romans 9:15, Paul quotes Jehovah God at the time when he promised to be gracious to Israelites involved in the sin with the golden calf: "I...will be gracious to whom I will be gracious, and will shew mercy on whom I will shew mercy" (Ex. 33:19). With regard to these people, all of whom were physical descendants of Abraham, all of whom were circumcised, all of whom were members of the earthly nation of Israel, and all of whom had been conceived and born guilty and totally depraved (worthy only of condemnation), God said that he would discriminate among them, being gracious and merciful only to some of them, not to all of them, and that the explanation was simply his eternal, predestinating will: "*to whom I will be gracious.*"

Romans 9 teaches that election governs the covenant and that the covenant realizes God's election.

What was true of the covenant in the Old Testament is true also today with regard particularly to God's salvation of the physical offspring of godly parents.

This the federal vision hates with a passion and rejects. It teaches the only alternative: The covenant, covenant grace, and covenant salvation depend on conditions that the children must perform, that is, on the will and works of the children.

Covenant salvation depends on the children. What governs the covenant is the will of the sinner, particularly the will of sinful little children and young people.

This is the Arminian heresy applied to the covenant.

What does the federal vision do with Romans 9? Outwardly, the men of the federal vision ignore it or explain it away as referring to a temporal, changeable, conditional choice of God, responding to children's performing or failing to perform conditions. Inwardly, the men of the federal vision gnash their teeth at Romans 9, that it was ever written and included in the Bible. Because the Canons of Dordt confess the truth of God's sovereignty in salvation that is taught in Romans 9, the men of the federal vision gnash their teeth at the Canons of Dordt as well. They express their opposition to the Canons by disparaging "systematic theology" and praising "biblical theology."[4] The systematic theology of the Canons of Dordt, however, is solidly based on the biblical theology of Romans 9.

With regard to the teaching of the federal vision, how does the rejection of Esau harmonize with its teaching of grace to Esau? Since Esau was hated by God, how could God make a well-meant offer of salvation to him?

This question is based on Romans 9:13: "Jacob have I loved, but Esau have I hated."

In Romans 9, the text reveals God's attitude toward Esau before he was born or had done any evil (v. 11). It is revelation of God's eternal reprobation, or rejection, of Esau unto damnation in God's hatred of him, that is, his detestation of Esau and will that Esau perish everlastingly. Esau, the apostle notes, was a child of believing parents, a grandchild of the father of believers, Abraham, and circumcised with the Old Testament equivalent of New Testament baptism.

However the men of the federal vision may explain the text away, or ignore it (as do countless other Reformed

4   Don Garlington, "Covenantal Nomism and the Exile," in *A Faith That Is Never Alone*, 391.

and Presbyterian theologians, ministers, and laymen today), the text is the inspired contradiction of a basic tenet of the federal vision, namely, that God shows covenant grace to all the physical children of godly parents alike and that God even begins to bestow covenant grace upon them all alike. Behind this, of course, is supposed to be a gracious attitude toward all the children alike and a gracious desire to save them all alike.

The Holy Spirit, however, states that God hated Esau from eternity and willed *not* to have mercy on him (which God owes to no child of believing parents, nor anyone else for that matter). To teach that God was gracious to Esau—to teach that he had the same covenant grace for Esau that he had for Jacob—is to contradict Romans 9:13, to subvert the system of theology known as Calvinism, and to overthrow the gospel of grace, of which the truth of reprobation is an essential element.

As verse 15 of Romans 9 will state (not imply, but explicitly state) about circumcised offspring of Abraham in the Old Testament (and about baptized children of believers in the New Testament), God in his sovereignty has (covenant) mercy, not upon all alike, but upon whom he wills to have mercy. Romans 9:6–23 teaches, and was exactly intended to teach, that covenant grace is particular and sovereign, not universal and resistible, that is, conditioned on the will, worth, and works of covenant children.

The question assumes that there is a close relation between the covenant theology of the federal vision and the doctrine of a well-meant offer of salvation. The assumption is correct. I will explain the relation more thoroughly in my answer to another question specifically about the relation. Here I observe that the doctrine of a well-meant offer is the teaching that God has a gracious attitude toward all who hear the preaching of the gospel, sincerely desiring to save them all, and that in this grace he offers Christ and salvation to all alike, reprobate as well as elect (if the proponents of the well-meant offer even believe eternal reprobation). The advocates of the well-meant offer hold, in the language of Romans 9:13, that God had a gracious attitude toward Esau, as well as toward Jacob; that

God sincerely desired Esau's salvation, as well as Jacob's; and that by the circumcision of Esau and by the word of God that Esau's parents undoubtedly taught the boy, God was graciously offering Esau salvation.

The doctrine of the federal vision, as well as the doctrine of a conditional covenant that it is developing, goes the teaching of the well-meant offer one worse. It has God being gracious toward Esau (and all other children born to believing parents who are reprobate and perish) and desirous of Esau's salvation, just as does the doctrine of a well-meant offer. But whereas the well-meant offer has God making a conditional, resistible, gracious offer to those who perish, the federal vision has God making a conditional, resistible, gracious *promise* to those who perish.

The well-meant offer wreaks havoc on God's gospel-call.

The federal vision wreaks havoc on God's solemn, oath-bound promise.

The former makes God impotent.

The latter makes God a liar.

Romans 9:11–13 exposes both teachings as false.

> (For the children being not yet born, neither having done any good or evil, that the purpose of God according to election might stand, not of works, but of him that calleth;) It was said unto her, The elder shall serve the younger. As it is written, Jacob have I loved, but Esau have I hated.

Have the men of the federal vision responded to the charge that their doctrine of a conditional covenant with all the children of believers is in conflict with Romans 9:6, 13: "They are not all Israel, which are of Israel"; "Jacob have I loved, but Esau have I hated"?

They have no response to the clear, compelling teaching of Romans 9:6–33 that the covenant promise to Abraham concerning his seed and the covenant itself are particular and that this particularity is determined by God's eternal election of grace: "That the purpose of God according to election might stand" (v. 11). "I will have mercy on whom I will have mercy" (v. 15).

They are very leery of even attempting a response *that addresses the objections to their covenant doctrine based on Romans 9 and that offers an explanation of the passage, taking into account the understanding of the passage by the Reformed creeds, especially the Canons of Dordt.* In fact, the regnant explanation of Romans 9 by the men of the federal vision is that of the new perspective on Paul. That is, Martin Luther, John Calvin, and the Reformed confessions misunderstood Paul, especially in Romans 9, which does not teach that the covenant is governed by eternal election. Rather, Romans 9 teaches that a gracious covenant made by God with all the children of believers, Esau as truly as Jacob, *conditionally,* governs a temporal, changeable election of children that is dependent on their performing conditions. Incidentally, this is no new perspective on Paul. It is an old perspective on Paul. It is the perspective on Paul that the semi-Pelagians and Arminians have had for centuries.

Romans 9, as authoritatively (and rightly) explained by the Reformed creeds, is *the* rock upon which the universal, resistible grace of the federal vision's doctrine of a conditional covenant with all the children alike is dashed.

In 1 Peter 1:18–20, the apostle Peter asserts, "Ye know that ye were...redeemed...with the precious blood of Christ." The Canons of Dordt teach the same truth: redemption through the precious blood of Jesus Christ alone (Canons 2, "Of the Death of Christ, and the Redemption of Men thereby"). Does the federal vision mentality deny that God's elect know they were redeemed (and, therefore, are in the covenant of grace) through the precious blood of Christ alone?

In opposition to Canons 2.8, the men of the federal vision deny that Christ confirmed the new covenant by dying in the place of, and redeeming, the elect, and the elect only, according to the eternal counsel of election.

According to the men of the federal vision, Christ died for all humans without exception, particularly for all the baptized children of godly parents without exception. (In the theology of the federal vision, all the physical offspring of godly parents are elect at birth and baptism; however, any and all of them may become reprobate later in life by failing to perform the conditions of the covenant.)

Criticizing Calvinism's restriction to "only...the elect" of the "saving love of God revealed in the atonement" that John 3:16 proclaims, Norman Shepherd declares: "The Reformed evangelist can and must preach to everyone on the basis of John 3:16, 'Christ died to save you.'" When Shepherd adds in explanation that "John 3:16 is covenant truth," he makes plain that in his (federal vision) theology, the death of Christ established, or made possible the establishment of, a conditional covenant of grace, not only with all the infants of godly parents, but also with all humans without exception.[5]

According to Shepherd, Christ died not only for all baptized children without exception—Esau as well as Jacob—but also for all humans without exception. He died for all to establish the covenant of grace with all. But both the cross and the covenant are conditional.

What the difference might be between this doctrine of the death of Christ in relation to the covenant and that condemned by the Canons of Dordt in the rejection of errors section of the second head of the Canons, neither Shepherd nor any other federal vision theologian has yet attempted to demonstrate.

From Norman Shepherd, John Frame learned that God loved all the circumcised children of Israel in the Old Testament and that he loves all the baptized children of believers in the New Testament with the love of John 3:16—a love that Frame recognizes "sent his Son to die." This love for all the children

5   Shepherd, *Call of Grace*, 84–85.

without exception—the love of John 3:16, expressed in the death of Christ—is the "covenant of love" of Deuteronomy 7.[6] Like the theology of the conditional covenant that it is developing and like the theology of Arminianism, of which it is a reworked form (Arminianism is essentially a gospel of conditional salvation), the federal vision teaches that the death of Christ merely permits God to establish his covenant with all the physical offspring of believers alike, uniting them all to Christ; giving grace to all of them so that they can perform the conditions, if only they are willing; and bestowing upon them all the blessings of the covenant, including justification.

All of the children for the first few years of their life can and should know that Christ died to redeem them. He did die to redeem them all, according to the federal vision and the conditional doctrine of the covenant that the federal vision is developing. But this does not mean that they will surely be saved. All of them can fall away and perish.

The same is true of adult believers.

The theology of the federal vision denies that the death of Christ was limited in extent; was the perfect satisfaction of the justice of God for those, and those only, for whom he died; and was effectual to save every one in whose stead Christ died. The federal vision denies the cross of Christ. It denies the cross of Christ particularly with regard to the covenant and the baptized children of believing parents.

In the language of 1 Peter 1:18–20, the teaching of the federal vision is something like this: "You know, at the present time (while you are performing the conditions of the covenant), that you were redeemed with the blood of Christ (but in reality the blood of Christ did not redeem anybody; it only made redemption possible for those who perform the conditions to their last gasp). Do not suppose, however, that this knowledge assures you of everlasting life. Many who know for a while that they were redeemed with the blood of Christ later fail to perform the conditions of the covenant and perish in hell. The same may

6   Frame, *Doctrine of God*, 418–19.

happen to you, if you fail to perform the conditions, and it is very well possible that you will fail to perform the conditions."

How would the men of the federal vision explain Cain and Abel?

The federal vision explains Cain and Abel (Gen. 4) just as it explains all other children of believing parents. God was gracious to both of them alike, desirous of saving both of them. In his common, covenant grace, God began in them the work of saving both of them. But at the decisive moment in their lives, Abel performed the required condition—faith and obedience—upon which the continuation of his covenant salvation depended, and was saved, whereas Cain refused to perform the condition and perished.

The federal vision reads Hebrews 11:4 this way: "By the performance of the work of believing, Abel offered unto God a more excellent sacrifice than Cain, because of which faith and obedience he made himself righteous with God, thus distinguishing himself from his brother."

According to the federal vision, Cain lost his salvation, and Abel's salvation depended upon Abel. In the case of the former, God was defeated; in the case of the latter, he was dependent.

THE FEDERAL VISION AND
THE COVENANT WITH ADAM   9

Federal vision theology denies that God's covenant relationship with Adam was a covenant of works, that in justification the merits of Christ's righteousness are imputed to the believer, and that merit of any kind is the basis of salvation. Protestant Reformed theology also denies that God's covenant relationship with Adam was a covenant of works and generally emphasizes the sovereign grace of election as the basis of salvation, more than the merits of Christ as imputed to the believer. Where is the merit of Christ in your understanding of the covenant of grace?

My understanding of Protestant Reformed theology is that it teaches that the grace of election is the *source*, or *fountain*, of all salvation, including covenant salvation. The cross of Christ, by which he merited salvation for all whom the Father has given him, is the legal *basis* of salvation in the covenant. To my mind we do not emphasize one more than the other—fountain more than basis. In fact, in accordance with 1 Corinthians 2:2, our message is "Jesus Christ, and him crucified." But we do not preach the cross as justification apart from, much less in opposition to, the eternal, gracious election of God, whence that cross with its justifying and sanctifying benefits proceeds.

The merits of Christ are the legal basis of the covenant of grace, as they are the righteousness of the member of the covenant. God established the new covenant in the blood of the cross. Divine justice required that Jesus Christ merit the covenant, its blessings, and its salvation for the elect, covenant people. This Jesus did by his lifelong obedience to the law in the stead of his people and especially by voluntarily paying to God the debt of the guilt of his people's sins by his atoning suffering and death. "Then I restored that which I took not away" (Ps. 69:4).

Many men of the federal vision deny that Christ merited salvation for his people and that in justification the believer (by faith) receives the merits of Christ. In these denials they stand condemned by the Reformed confessions. Article 22 of the Belgic Confession, for instance, teaches that "Jesus Christ, imputing to us all his merits, and so many holy works, which he hath done for us and in our stead, is our Righteousness."[1]

In addition, the question asks about the apparent similarity of the theology of the federal vision and the theology of the Protestant Reformed Churches regarding the covenant with Adam. Both deny that the covenant with Adam was a "covenant of works" *in the sense of a covenant in which Adam was supposed to, or ever could, earn for himself and all the human race the higher, better, immortal, spiritual, heavenly, eternal life that, in fact, Jesus earned for the elect church by his redeeming death.*

The apparent similarity of teaching with regard to this one, particular aspect of their theologies ought to deceive no one. Nor will any theologian possessed of acuity and honesty ever appeal to this apparent similarity in order to suggest to the public that there is basic agreement between the theology of the federal vision and the theology of the Protestant Reformed Churches. The similarity is mostly apparent, not real. For, first, the rejection by the federal vision of the notion that Adam could merit eternal life is an aspect of the federal vision's denial of the meritorious work of Jesus Christ. The Protestant Reformed Churches, in contrast, emphatically teach the meritorious nature of the covenant work of Jesus Christ.

Second, although the federal vision denies that Adam could have merited eternal life, it teaches that Adam could,

---

1   Belgic Confession, Art. 22, in *Creeds of Christendom*, 3:408.

nevertheless, have *obtained* eternal life for himself and all his posterity by his obedience. Following the bizarre, allegorical exegesis of James Jordan, some of the theologians of the federal vision speak of Adam's *maturing into* eternal life, so that one day he might have been permitted to eat of the fruit of the tree of the knowledge of good and evil.[2]

The Protestant Reformed Churches deny that Adam could have obtained eternal life in any way or by any means. By virtue of God's decree and of his own unique status and ability as the eternal Son of God in human flesh, Jesus Christ, and Jesus Christ *alone*, could, might, and did obtain eternal life for himself and his body, the church. He did this by incarnation, cross, and resurrection in the power of the Holy Spirit, who was given to him without measure.

The one real similarity between the two theologies regarding the covenant with Adam is that both view that covenant not as a cold, businesslike contract, but as a warm, living bond of communion in love. This has been the theology of covenant of the Protestant Reformed Churches for more than eighty years. The men of the federal vision have very recently come to this understanding; how, they do not tell us.

Regarding this one aspect of the covenant theology of the federal vision from which the broader Reformed community could profitably learn, the federal vision is mercilessly hammered by the Reformed and Presbyterian defenders of the faith, as though this were the federal vision's greatest, if not only, covenant iniquity.

Doesn't Christ's meriting by perfect obedience imply a covenant of works, at least between the Father and the Son, that Christ fulfilled?

This question addresses two important aspects of the controversy in the Reformed churches occasioned by the federal vision. First, the men of the federal vision reject the teaching that

2 See James B. Jordan, "Merit Versus Maturity: What Did Jesus Do for Us?" in *Federal Vision*, 158–92.

Christ merited eternal life for his people. Not only do they oppose the doctrine that Adam could have merited eternal life, but they also oppose the doctrine that Christ merited. To teach that Christ had to merit with God, they argue, would be to teach an illegitimate covenant of works regarding the covenant established by Christ.

The second aspect of the controversy raised by this question is the counter-argument of those who defend a covenant of works with Adam, in which he could have merited a higher, spiritual, eternal life by obeying. Defenders of a meritorious covenant of works with Adam argue that, if Christ merited with God, so also Adam could have merited with God.

With regard to both aspects of the controversy over the federal vision that this question addresses, we must be clear what is meant by a covenant of works. By a covenant of works is meant a covenant between God and humans in which a mere man—a human, and nothing more than a human—can and must earn salvation, or eternal life, from God by his own obedience and works. (I am not here passing judgment on the meaning of the covenant of works in the Westminster standards; I am defining covenant of works as it is part of the controversy occasioned by the federal vision.)

Adam could not merit eternal life by his obedience in the garden. No mere man, not even a sinless mere man, can ever do more than is required of him so as to put God in his debt. For Adam as for us, the truth holds: "When ye shall have done all those things which are commanded you, say, We are unprofitable servants: we have done that which was our duty to do" (Luke 17:10).

First Corinthians 15:45–49 flatly denies that the first Adam could ever have bestowed on himself or on his descendants anything more than "natural" life. He was "earthy." Only the "Lord from heaven" can give humans "spiritual" and "heavenly" life, that is, the eternal life that the risen Jesus Christ gives his own by his Spirit. Adam could give the race "the image of the earthy" (apart now from the decree that he fall to make way for Christ). Only Jesus Christ can give the "image of the heavenly."

God himself could not give Adam the privilege of meriting (by virtue of the covenant, as they argue), because God cannot deny himself: He cannot put himself in the debt of mere man; he cannot pay mere men eternal life as wages due them. Man must always be indebted to God; God can never be indebted to man. For God to be indebted to mere man would be the "ungodding" of God.

The covenant with Adam in paradise was not a covenant of works *in the sense of a meritorious covenant.*

I have written more extensively about the covenant with Adam in previous chapters in this book and also in an article that is readily available to those who are interested, and I need not say more about the subject here.[3]

The second aspect of the question concerns the covenant established in Jesus Christ, specifically whether Christ's obedience was meritorious and, if it was, whether this implies that the covenant Christ established by merit is, in fact, a covenant of works.

About the denial by the federal vision that Christ's obedience was meritorious, I can be brief. Denying that Christ's obedience merited, or earned, eternal life with God, the men of the federal vision stand condemned by the Reformed and Presbyterian creeds.

Article 22 of the Belgic Confession declares that true, justifying faith "embraces Jesus Christ with all his merits."[4]

Against the Arminian (and federal vision) heresy that those once united to Christ (enjoying "the communion of...Jesus Christ"[5]) can fall away and perish eternally, the Canons of Dordt object that this is "utterly impossible," among other reasons, "since...the merit...of Christ [cannot] be rendered ineffectual."[6]

3   David J. Engelsma, "The Covenant of Creation with Adam" *Protestant Reformed Theological Journal* 40, no. 1 (November 2006): 3–42.

4   Belgic Confession, Art. 22, in *Creeds of Christendom*, 3:408.

5   Canons of Dordt, 5.1, in ibid., 3:592.

6   Canons of Dordt, 5.8, in ibid., 3:594.

Almost all of the men of the federal vision are members of confessionally Reformed churches and have, therefore, solemnly promised to uphold and never to criticize the teachings of the creeds. When they oppose the doctrine of the meritorious obedience of Christ, they break their vow. Their churches must not argue with them but discipline them.

It should also be noted in passing that the denial by the federal vision that the obedience of Christ was meritorious is part and parcel of their comprehensive attack on the truth that salvation is importantly legal: God's imputation of the guilt of the elect to Christ; Christ's legal representation of the elect in the whole of his lifelong obedience to the will of God; and God's imputation of Christ's obedience to the elect sinner by faith alone. An attack on the legal aspect of salvation is an attack on the righteousness of God.

Christ could and did merit with God because he is not only a real man, but also God himself. God can merit with God, just as God can satisfy the justice of God and God can bear, so as to bear away, the wrath of God. It was God in human flesh who merited with God, but the person of the one who merited is God the eternal Son.

As God himself, with regard to his person, and as a perfectly sinless man not responsible for Adam's disobedience, Christ restored that which he took not away (Ps. 69:4). The eternal Son in our flesh did that which he was not obliged to do, and thus God in Christ merited—*earned*—for us deliverance from death and the highest, eternal life.

Christ had to merit. Meriting was necessary, because the justice of God demanded full payment for sin and adequate basis for inheriting eternal life. Merit is due to divine justice. Repudiation of merit (on the part of Christ) is denial of the righteousness of God.

That Christ merited does not imply that the covenant of God with him and with those who belong to him (Gal. 3:16, 29) is a covenant of works. Covenant of works describes a covenant in which *mere man* earns with God. The meritorious nature of Christ's lifelong obedience, culminating in the obedience of the atoning death of Christ, rather magnifies the grace of the covenant with Christ and his people. What we sinners could not do for ourselves, God himself accomplished for us and in our place in Jesus Christ. This is grace.

That Christ willingly obligated himself to merit eternal life for God's people no more makes the covenant between the triune God and himself, as the head of the covenant, a covenant of works than does the fact that Christ obligated himself to satisfy the demands of divine justice. *God was in Christ* establishing the covenant of grace by meriting, satisfying justice, and fulfilling every demand of the law. *Christ was God's willing servant* earning, paying, and submitting to divine justice. This is a covenant of grace—glorious grace.

The legal component of the covenant—meriting, meriting by hard labor, on the part of Christ—does not detract from grace; it extols grace.

Denying the meritorious nature of the lifelong obedience and satisfactory death of Christ, therefore, the men of the federal vision not only compromise the justice of God. They also sin against his grace.

THE FEDERAL VISION
AND COMMON GRACE 10

If there is no mercy or grace of God to the unbeliever, then for
what will they be judged and condemned by God?

The question is appropriate because it is the doctrine of the
men of the federal vision that there is a grace or mercy of God
to reprobate unbelievers—"real," covenant, saving grace or
mercy, a grace or mercy that consists of union with the risen
Christ and the possession and enjoyment (for a while) of the
benefits of salvation in him.

The Bible teaches that there is no mercy of God to the reprobate
unbeliever. Quoting God's own word to Moses in Exodus
33:19, "[I] will be gracious to whom I will be gracious, and
will shew mercy on whom I will shew mercy," Paul wrote in
Romans 9:15: "I will have mercy on whom I will have mercy,
and I will have compassion on whom I will have compassion."
The context in Romans 9 makes plain that God's mercy has its
source in, and is determined by, his election of some accompanied by his reprobation of others. Verse 23, explaining who
receives the discriminating mercy, says, "the vessels which he
had afore prepared unto glory."

The two passages, Exodus 33 and Romans 9, directly address
the heresy of the federal vision, for the federal vision teaches
that God is merciful in his covenant dealings with all the physical children of believing parents alike, those who ultimately go
lost as well as those who finally are saved. In Exodus 33 and
Romans 9, Scripture teaches that the covenant mercy of God is

particular. With reference to the people of Israel, all of whom were physical descendants of Abraham, circumcised (leaving aside the Egyptian hangers-on), and in the sphere of the covenant, God himself declares in Exodus 33 that he has mercy on whom he wills to have mercy. God's mercy is discriminating. It is not for all the physical offspring of Abraham. Paul repeats this truth in Romans 9, applying it by implication to the physical offspring of believers.

Contrary to the federal vision, the covenant mercy of God, with regard specifically to the children of believers, is particular not general. God himself says so. And what determines the objects of his covenant mercy is not the worthiness of certain children in distinction from others or that some distinguish themselves from others by performing conditions. What determines the objects of covenant mercy is eternal, unconditional, gracious election in Christ.

The Canons of Dordt teach that the grace of God is particular, that is, for the elect alone:

> According to which [the one decree of election] he hath chosen us from eternity, both to grace and to glory.[1]

> Election is the fountain of every saving good; from which proceed faith, holiness, and the other gifts of salvation, and finally eternal life itself, as its fruits and effects.[2]

The Canons condemn as an Arminian error the teaching that God did not "pass anyone by in the communication of grace which is necessary for faith and conversion."[3]

This is the error that the federal vision is teaching today. The federal vision teaches that God is gracious at baptism to all the physical children of believers alike, those who will perish as well as those who finally are saved. At and by baptism, God bestows grace as a power and as spiritual gifts upon every child. And when a child grows up and fails to perform the

---

1   Canons of Dordt, 1.8, in *Creeds of Christendom*, 3:583.

2   Canons of Dordt, 1.9, in ibid., 3:583.

3   Canons of Dordt, 1, Rejection of Errors 8, in *Confessions and Church Order*, 162.

conditions that are necessary to stay in the covenant and be saved by it, that child loses and forfeits real grace that he had received from God.

If some baptized persons are never the objects of God's favorable attitude or the recipients of God's saving power, that is, covenant grace, on what ground are they condemned for their unbelief and disobedience?

The impenitent unbeliever who is raised in the sphere of the covenant, as a baptized child of believers and as one who was taught the gospel, like someone on the mission field who rejected the gospel, does indeed sin against the grace of God in Jesus Christ, is indeed guilty of unbelief regarding the gospel of grace, and does indeed insult the Spirit of grace (Heb. 10:29). God will condemn him for despising and rejecting his grace and for despising and rejecting Jesus Christ himself. Such an unbeliever's judgment will be heavier than that of Sodom or of the heathen who live and die completely ignorant of the gospel.

The ground of the condemnation will be that grace and Christ were presented and made known to him in the preaching and teaching of the gospel, as well as in the sacrament of baptism, which was administered to him. In addition, God seriously commanded him to repent and believe the gospel, which is his duty and which he knows to be his duty.

But the ground of God's judgment of the reprobate ungodly in the sphere of the covenant will not be that God on his part had a gracious attitude toward them and even began the work of grace and salvation in them. To teach this is, in addition to contradicting Exodus 33, Romans 9, and the Canons of Dordt 1.8–9, to teach universal, conditional, resistible grace: the Arminian heresy. And the doctrine of universal, conditional, resistible grace implies that those who are saved are not saved by the power of the grace of God, but by their own will.

One can despise and reject Jesus Christ crucified even though Jesus Christ was not crucified for him personally. One can insult, or in the words of the Authorized Version in Hebrews 10:29, "do despite unto," the Spirit of grace even though the Spirit never regenerated or indwelled him. One can break the covenant even though the covenant was never established with him personally. So one can despise and reject the saving, covenant grace of God in Jesus Christ without personally being the object or recipient of grace.

To insist that if someone will be judged for despising grace he must, in reality, have been the object and recipient of grace is to hold that grace is universal, conditional, resistible, and losable. And this is the Arminian heresy.

Does the free, well-meant offer of the gospel necessarily lead to federal vision theology? Doesn't the doctrine of a free, well-meant offer of the gospel arise from the conditional covenant, which you say is the "root of the federal vision"?

The doctrine of a well-meant offer of the gospel is the teaching that the preaching of the gospel comes to all hearers *in the grace of God for them all alike* and *with the sincere desire of God to save them all*. The well-meant offer makes the (saving) grace of God wider than Christ and the elect in him. The well-meant offer cuts the grace of the preaching of the gospel loose from predestination. It denies that the source and fountain of the grace of God in the gospel is the divine election of a certain number of persons in Christ.

The doctrine of the preaching as a well-meant offer differs radically from the orthodox, Reformed doctrine of preaching as the presentation of Christ to all who hear, accompanied by the serious call (command) to all who hear to believe on this Christ and by the promise that all who do believe will be saved. This latter—the orthodox Reformed doctrine—is described in the Canons of Dordt as Christ's being "offered" and in the Westminster Confession of Faith as his being "freely offered."[4] "Offered" and "freely offered" in these Reformed confessions do not describe, and prescribe as Reformed orthodoxy, a universal grace of God in the preaching of the gospel, a (saving) grace cut loose from predestination, as everyone who can read the English language can see for himself by reading these two creeds.

4 Canons of Dordt, 3–4.9, in *Creeds of Christendom*, 3:589; Westminster Confession of Faith, 7.3, in ibid., 3:617.

Clever false teachers have introduced the heresy of universal, resistible grace into the Reformed churches, and vigorously defend the heresy today, by piggybacking the doctrine of a well-meant offer on the term "offer" in the confessions. A better figure is that they have made, and do make today, a Trojan horse of the term "offer." Inside this—in itself innocuous, in fact expressive, indeed creedal—term have been loaded a host of Arminian and Pelagian sentiments and teachings. By this time these aliens are devastating the Reformed city of God. Troy at least recognized the enemies and fought them, once the foes got out of the horse. Most of the Reformed churches welcome the sentiments and teachings of the well-meant offer as friends and allies.

Now to the question.

Historically, the doctrine of the well-meant offer arose out of the doctrine of a conditional covenant (which I do indeed affirm is the root of the federal vision). This took place in the Christian Reformed Church, whose role in spreading the doctrine of preaching as a well-meant offer throughout the Reformed and Presbyterian churches worldwide cannot be overestimated.

In 1924, at its synod of Kalamazoo, the Christian Reformed Church adopted the well-meant offer in the first of its three points of common grace. It described the general offer of the gospel as an expression of the grace of God for all humans alike and not exclusively for the elect. For rejecting this doctrine and condemning it as a form of Arminianism, that is, for defending the particularity and sovereignty of (saving) grace in the gospel, the Christian Reformed Church deposed and excommunicated ministers and consistories.[5] This was the beginning of the Protestant Reformed Churches, to their glory.

This stands as the shame and guilt of the Christian Reformed Church to this day.

---

5   For this history and the three points of common grace in which the Christian Reformed Church adopted the well-meant offer as official dogma, see Herman Hoeksema, *The Protestant Reformed Churches in America*, 2nd ed. (Grand Rapids, MI, 1947).

The Christian Reformed Church was led to adopt the well-meant offer because its seminary had been teaching ministers the doctrine of a conditional covenant for many years. The one chiefly responsible was Professor William Heyns. His covenant doctrine was that God is gracious to all the baptized children of believers alike; that the Reformed baptism form has all the children alike in view throughout; and that, in addition to his gracious attitude toward all the children alike, God actually bestows covenant grace, that is, inner, spiritual power, on all alike at baptism, so that all have the ability to fulfill the condition of faith, if only they are willing.[6]

Ministers reared on this covenant doctrine were ready to adopt the doctrine of a well-meant offer. They did at the synod of 1924.

Heyns' covenant doctrine is essentially the same as that of Klaas Schilder and the Reformed Churches in the Netherlands (liberated), now enthusiastically being developed by the federal vision. That Heyns' doctrine of the covenant is essentially the same as that of Schilder and the liberated churches is acknowledged by liberated theologian Jelle Faber: "The kinship of [Schilder] with the American Secession theologians, also with Heyns, came out [in Schilder's writings]"[7]

The relation works the other way round as well. Reformed and Presbyterian ministers reared on the well-meant offer will certainly not stumble at the teaching that God is gracious toward and desires to save, and even begins to bestow covenant grace upon, all the children of believing parents alike.

This explains the otherwise astounding fact that the federal vision can appear and make headway in confessedly Reformed churches—churches that confess the Canons of Dordt, which make election the cause and fountain of all grace, blessings, and salvation.

6   For Heyns' doctrine of the covenant and its influence on the adoption of the well-meant offer by the Christian Reformed Church, see Herman Hoeksema, *Believers and Their Seed*, 1–28.

7   Jelle Faber, *American Secession Theologians on Covenant and Baptism* (Neerlandia, AB, Canada: Inheritance Publications, 1996), 52. On the essential oneness of Schilder and Heyns, see 36–54.

This also explains the significant fact that, although some still object to the federal vision's denial of justification by faith alone, almost none (other than the Protestant Reformed Churches) make an issue of the federal vision's extension of saving, covenant grace *beyond the elect*. About this...*silence*. What the false doctrines of a well-meant offer and a conditional covenant have in common is this. Both cut the grace of salvation loose from election. Both teach a saving grace of God that is resistible, and resisted. Both teach, by clear and necessary implication, that those who are saved by the grace of the gospel and by the grace of the covenant are saved not by the irresistible power of the grace itself, but by their performance of the condition upon which the grace depends. Both agree, therefore, that certain objects of the grace of God in the gospel and of the covenant grace of God make themselves to differ from others by their acceptance of the gracious offer and their performance of the covenant conditions.

The apostle of grace denies this. "Who maketh thee to differ from another? and what hast thou that thou didst not receive? now if thou didst receive it, why dost thou glory, as if thou hadst not received it?" (1 Cor. 4:7).

How are the United Reformed Churches and other Reformed denominations to eradicate the root of the federal vision when they have not rejected the doctrine of common grace and, thus, do not adhere to the pure sovereignty of God?

Of course, these churches ought to get back to their doctrine of common grace too. But that is not the subject at present. The subject now is the federal vision, specifically the root of the federal vision. If these churches will seriously address the root of the federal vision—a gracious covenant promise to, the gracious establishment of the covenant with, and the bestowal of covenant blessings upon all the baptized children alike— they will also have to confront the issue of common grace, particularly, the teaching that God is gracious to all hearers in the preaching of the gospel (the well-meant offer of the gospel).

THE FEDERAL VISION AND THE BAPTISM FORM

Would you agree that the men of the federal vision misinterpreted the Reformed baptism form and believe the ceremony itself has the ability to bestow the covenant of grace? Was it this misconception that fostered the idea that people who leave the church—people who never had the covenant of grace—had fallen from grace?

I agree that the men of the federal vision, like the theologians and members of the Reformed Churches in the Netherlands (liberated) whose covenant doctrine the federal vision embraces and develops, misinterpret the baptism form. They explain the children of the form as being all the physical children without exception. From this it follows that the form teaches that all the children alike are again received unto grace in Christ, have been redeemed by the blood of Christ, are sanctified in Christ, and are indwelt by the Spirit. And this implies that some children fall away from the covenant grace of God and from Christ.

The men of the federal vision do indeed teach that the sacrament of baptism unites the baptized child very really to Christ—*every* baptized child—so that every baptized child receives the life and blessings of Christ. Because the continuation of the covenant and its salvation are conditional, however, every baptized child can lose grace, separate himself or herself from Christ, and perish eternally.

The fundamental error both of the federal vision and of the covenant theology of the Reformed Churches in the Netherlands (liberated), which is also the covenant theology today of other Reformed and Presbyterian churches, is that it does not allow election to govern the Reformed baptism form with regard to the covenant.

In the form for infant baptism we read, "When we baptize this child in the name of God the Father, he makes an eternal covenant of grace with this child." How can this be in the light of Scripture?

In the light of Scripture, this cannot be. And therefore, the Reformed baptism form does not, in fact, read like this. What the baptism form states is this: "When we are baptized in the name of the Father, God the Father witnesseth and sealeth unto us, that he doth make an eternal covenant of grace with us." What the form states concerning the children of believers is this: "Our young children...are...again received unto grace in Christ...[They] are to be baptized as heirs of the kingdom of God, and of his covenant."[1]

The reference of the baptism form to "us" is to elect believers, to elect believers only. The reference of the form to the "young children" and "infants" of believers, who are "again received unto grace in Christ," as "heirs of the kingdom of God, and of his covenant," is to the elect children of believers and the elect children only.

This understanding of those with whom God graciously establishes his covenant is faithful to the teaching of Scripture. According to Galatians 3:16, 29, when God promised to establish the covenant with Abraham's "seed," the reference was not to all of Abraham's physical descendants, was not to all those infants who received the sign of circumcision. Rather, the reference was to Christ and those who belong to Christ and to them only.

According to Romans 9:6–29, the seed of Abraham to whom the word of divine promise came, that God would establish his

1   Form for the Administration of Baptism, in *Confessions and Church Order*, 258–59.

covenant with them, bless them with the covenant blessings, and save them, were not all the physical offspring of Abraham. The covenant children of Abraham, rather, were those, and those only, among the physical offspring of Abraham whom God had eternally chosen in love and upon whom he willed to show compassion. So also, and for this biblical reason, the covenant children of believers in the baptism form, who are again received unto grace in Christ and to whom God seals his covenant by their baptism, are the elect children of godly parents and the elect children only. For them, and them only, is the sacrament a means of grace.

This question about the baptism form is extremely important in the present controversy over the covenant raised by the federal vision. The federal vision is promoting and developing the covenant doctrine of the Reformed Churches in the Netherlands (liberated) and of their daughter and sister churches in North America and elsewhere. This covenant doctrine explains the children in the Reformed baptism form as all the physical offspring of believers alike. With all alike, God establishes the eternal covenant of grace. To all alike, the Son witnesses that he washes them from all their sins. The Spirit assures all alike that he is willing to dwell in them and will dwell in them. All alike are again received unto grace in Christ. All alike are heirs of the kingdom and covenant of God. All alike are sanctified in Christ. All alike have been forgiven all their sins by the blood of Christ, are received as members of Christ, and are adopted as children of God.

Conditionally!

If this explanation of the baptism form is correct, the theology of the federal vision is soundly Reformed, and nothing can be charged against it.

Yes, and then Dordt was a gigantic and miserable mistake.

Yes, and then the whole of the Reformed gospel of salvation by sovereign (irresistible), particular grace is exposed as false.

Yes, and the day I am convinced of this, I make my way back to Rome in sackcloth and ashes.

One benefit of the heresy of the federal vision for Reformed churches, ministers, and believers can be, and ought to be, that they study with renewed interest the Reformed baptism form. In a book that has recently been published, I take up in two chapters the crucial issue of the meaning of the Reformed baptism form, particularly its reference to the children of believers and its statement that our children are "sanctified in Christ."[2]

We also read in one of the forms, "Whereas in all covenants, there are contained two parts: therefore are we by God through baptism admonished of, and obliged unto, new obedience." Does not the form lead into federal vision theology? Is the form a Trojan horse?

The quotation is from the Reformed baptism form. The doctrine that the form teaches by this statement does not lead toward the theology of the federal vision. Containing this statement and doctrine, the form is not a Trojan horse in the Reformed camp, subtly carrying the enemy of grace into the intimate, sacramental life of the congregation and of the family.

Obedience to God is our "part" in the covenant, not our work upon which the covenant, its continued blessings, and its salvation depend, or by which some distinguish themselves from others equally furnished with covenant grace. That is, "part" is not "condition."

By virtue of the very nature of the covenant as fellowship in love between God and his people, the covenant people have a God-assigned "part" in the covenant. And it is an aspect of God's unconditional promise of the covenant to those who are Christ's by eternal election that God will work the doing of his or her part in every one with whom he establishes the covenant. "I will put my law in their inward parts, and write it in their hearts" (Jer. 31:33). When we do our part, willingly and without compulsion, as God demands, we confess that God works in us the willing and the doing (Phil. 2:13).

2   See chapter 2, "The Reformed Baptism Form: 'Received unto Grace in Christ,'" and especially chapter 3, "The Reformed Baptism Form: 'Sanctified in Christ,'" in Engelsma, *Covenant and Election*, 33–62.

The motive with which we heed the admonition to do our part is gratitude for gracious, covenant salvation. The motive is not the arrogant purpose of making an inherently uncertain covenant sure for ourselves. Nor is the motive terror lest by failing to keep conditions we lose the covenant, its grace, and its salvation.

At the same time Reformed ministers and church members may not so react against the federal vision and its doctrine of a conditional covenant that they fail to do full justice to the teaching of the baptism form (which is the teaching of Scripture everywhere) that they have a part in the covenant; that they have a duty to be active in the covenant; that they are admonished to be active in the covenant; and that their active part is obedience—full, unconditional, self-sacrificing obedience.

If we ministers do not preach this, we are derelict in our calling as preachers of the covenant of grace.

If a baptized child, or a baptized and confessing adult for that matter, disobeys, persistently and impenitently, he tramples the covenant underfoot (which is the sense of "covenant breaking" in the Bible), shows himself to be no member of the covenant at all, and perishes under the heaviest wrath of God. This too must be preached.

"And if we sometimes through weakness fall into sin, we must not therefore despair of God's mercy, nor continue in sin, since baptism is a seal and undoubted testimony that we have an eternal covenant of grace with God."[3]

Is not infant baptism a work toward salvation?

This is obviously the question of one who reacts against the doctrine and practice of infant baptism, which features so prominently in the controversy with the federal vision, by rejecting infant baptism altogether.

But this is as unwise as it would be to reject the sacrament of the Lord's supper because the errors of Rome and Lutheranism have made it controversial.

---

3   Form for the Administration of Baptism, in *Confessions and Church Order*, 258.

Infant baptism is no more a "work" toward salvation than adult baptism is a "work" toward salvation.

Infant baptism is a Christ-ordained sign and seal of the righteousness of faith applied to infants of believers because God commands it (Gen. 17:9–14), because of the covenant between God and the infants of believers (Gen. 17:7; Acts 2:39), and because Jesus told us to allow the infants to come to him (Luke 18:15–17). The ceremony is obviously not a work of the infant, because he or she is passive in the administration of the sacrament. But the sacrament is the work of God. It is a sign of God's salvation of the infants—*in their infancy*. It is a means of grace to the (elect) children, as soon as they are old enough to hear and understand the gospel, to assure them of the pardon of sins in the blood of Christ and to renew them to holiness of life.

THE FEDERAL VISION AND COVENANT CHILDREN 12

What is the promise of the covenant to which godly parents must cling while raising their children?

The covenant promise to believing parents is the solemn oath of God that he will save their children by the Spirit of Christ, usually already in their infancy, on the basis of the death of Christ for them and because of his eternal election of them in grace. "I will establish my covenant between me and thee and thy seed after thee in their generations for an everlasting covenant, to be a God unto thee, and to thy seed after thee" (Gen. 17:7). As the Reformed baptism form states, this promise, which was first made to Abraham, God now speaks "unto us and our children." The baptism form also explains this promise as meaning that the "young children" of believers are, without their knowledge, "received unto grace in Christ."[1] This is salvation by the Spirit of Christ, on the basis of the cross, according to election.

This promise does not necessarily refer to all of the children of godly parents. It may. Often it does, because God in his grace has elected all the children of particular godly parents. But there may be reprobate children among the physical children of godly parents. The covenant promise does not refer to the reprobate offspring. Only the elect in Christ are the true, spiritual children of believers, and the covenant promise is personally addressed to, and refers to, them only.

1 Form for the Administration of Baptism, in *Confessions and Church Order*, 259.

God teaches this in Romans 9:6–33. They are not all children of godly parents who are of godly parents, just as they were not all Israel who were of Israel. Only the children of the promise are counted for the seed of godly parents, just as only the children of the promise were counted for the seed of Abraham, to whom the word of God's covenant promise referred. And the children of the promise are those whom God graciously elected in Christ, in distinction from those whom God eternally reprobated outside of Christ.

God also impresses upon parents that ordinarily he is pleased to carry out the covenant promise in the way of the parents' prayers for their children; in the way of the Christian rearing of the children in the home, at church, and in good Christian schools; in the way of the godly disciplining of the children; and in the way of the parents' example to their children of the Christian life.

Clinging to the promise and pleading the promise, godly parents receive their children from God *as his children* and, however imperfectly, carry out their calling to rear the children God has given them. For the salvation of their children, the parents thank God fervently, confessing that their own efforts at rearing, though faithful by God's grace in the parents, can save none of them.

If one or more of the children, nevertheless, show themselves unbelieving, the parents continue to pray for them and to admonish them. The parents do not criticize God. He owes salvation to no one. And it pleases him to display the sovereignty of his grace in the saving of some children against the background of his righteous damning of others. Parents certainly do not charge against him that the word of his covenant promise failed, whether because he was powerless or he lied. "Not as though the word of God hath taken none effect" (Rom. 9:6).

If parents have been disobedient and careless in the rearing of the children who grow up showing themselves unbelieving and disobedient, having failed to instruct diligently, having neglected to discipline or having disciplined harshly, and having set an example to their children of ungodly behavior, the parents have themselves to blame for the spiritual and eternal death of their own flesh and blood.

Predestination in the sphere of the covenant does not destroy or weaken covenant responsibility, particularly with regard to the rearing of the children. It establishes responsibility, whether good rearing as the means of covenant salvation or bad rearing that brings down heavy and very painful judgment.

Nor may the children presume on the promise: "Even though I rebel against my parents, leave the church, and impenitently live in disobedience to the law of God, I am saved and may expect to go to heaven when I die; I am a covenant child." So long as a baptized child of believing parents lives thus impenitently in unbelief and disobedience, he or she must regard himself or herself as a covenant breaker (violator), upon whom the wrath of God falls more heavily than upon Sodom, and who will certainly be damned, the water of baptism forever sizzling on his or her forehead.

Genuine covenant children can, and do, have and enjoy the salvation of the promise (sealed to them by their baptism) only by faith, and faith produces the covenant life of holiness. Godly parents instruct their children from earliest years that the only way of salvation for them, as for their parents, is faith in the promising God in Jesus Christ. The covenant promise works this faith in them.

What is the essential difference between teaching that children of believers are in the covenant or that they are merely in the sphere, or realm, of the covenant? Suppose that a godly young couple sits in the front of church for the baptism of their infant child. Is that child in the covenant? In his commentary on the Heidelberg Catechism, Ursinus speaks of "conditions" in connection with the phrase "in baptism." Is there a carefully nuanced way to speak of a conditional covenant?

There are several distinct aspects to this question.

First, the three forms of unity, which are the authoritative creeds of the Protestant Reformed Churches, as of many other Reformed denominations, do not speak of conditions of salvation or of conditions of the covenant. On the contrary, they explicitly *condemn* the term "condition" in connection with election, salvation, and the covenant.[2]

Second, it is not only important, but also necessary to distinguish two kinds of relationships to the covenant on the part of the physical children of godly parents. The Bible makes this distinction in Romans 9:6 regarding the physical, circumcised children of Abraham. Some are merely "of Israel"; others are "Israel." It is this distinction, nothing more and nothing less, that Reformed orthodoxy makes by its teaching that some children are in the covenant internally, whereas others are in the covenant merely externally; or that some children are in the covenant, whereas others are merely under the administration of the covenant; or in the language I prefer that some are members of the covenant, whereas others are merely in the sphere of the covenant.

This difference, Romans 9 reveals, is due to God's eternal election of some—those who are "Israel," or members of the covenant—in distinction from others whom he has reprobated—those merely "of Israel," or in the sphere of the covenant.

To refuse to make this biblical distinction between two kinds of physical children of believing parents, to insist that all the children are alike covenant children of God—alike objects of the gracious covenant promise, alike united to Christ, alike the beneficiaries in their infancy of the covenant blessings of salvation, indeed, alike graciously elected by God—as is the covenant doctrine of the federal vision, is to teach resistible (covenant) grace, the falling away of (covenant) saints, and the dependency of God for (covenant) salvation upon the children. It is utterly to overthrow the system of doctrine of the Canons of Dordt, that is, the gospel of sovereign grace.

---

2   Canons of Dordt, 1.9–10, in *Creeds of Christendom*, 3:583; Canons of Dordt, 1, Rejection of Errors 2–5, 7, in *Confessions and Church Order*, 160–62; Canons of Dordt, 2, Rejection of Errors 3, in ibid., 165; and Canons of Dordt, 5, Rejection of Errors 1, in ibid., 176.

Third, the godly couple presenting their infant for baptism ought to regard their child as a covenant child, that is, as a member of the covenant, and not merely as a child who is in the sphere of the covenant. They must rear that child as a covenant child. So also ought the congregation to view the child and do their part in the instruction of the child. This is sometimes called the "judgment of charity." It is more than a judgment of charity. It is the judgment of charity that is *grounded in the covenant of God with believers and their children.* It is the judgment of the covenant.

Emphatically, parents and congregation must not view and treat the child as a little, unregenerated viper. To view, and then to treat, the infant of the godly couple at the baptismal font as an unregenerated, unsaved child of Satan, whose spiritual state and condition are no different from those of idolatrous heathen, is egregious disregard for and contradiction of everything infant baptism represents and everything the inclusion of the children of believers in the covenant with their parents signifies.

But this does not mean that the godly parents and the congregation can be absolutely sure that that particular child is an elect, saved child of God. God does not give them this knowledge. They do not need this knowledge. They may not have this knowledge. Only God knows those who are his—*and the elect, saved child of God himself or herself knows,* by faith. "Nevertheless the foundation of God standeth sure, having this seal, The Lord knoweth them that are his" (2 Tim. 2:19).

> The elect...attain the assurance of this their eternal and unchangeable election...by observing in themselves... the infallible fruits of election pointed out in the Word of God.[3]

It is exactly this view of the infants of believers that the Canons make confessional in article 17 of the first head.

> Since we are to judge of the will of God from his Word, which testifies that the children of believers are holy,

---

3 Canons of Dordt, 1.12, in *Creeds of Christendom*, 3:583–84.

not by nature, but in virtue of the covenant of grace, in which they together with the parents are comprehended, godly parents have no reason to doubt of the election and salvation of their children whom it pleaseth God to call out of this life in their infancy.[4]

We view the children as elect, saved children of God, by virtue of the covenant, and will then certainly rear those who survive infancy as such. But this is not the presumption of absolute certainty concerning their election and salvation. "Have no reason to doubt" is not the same as "are absolutely certain."

The men of the federal vision, and other defenders of a conditional covenant of grace with all the children alike, charge against this aspect of the doctrine of an unconditional covenant with the elect children that it destroys the certainty of parents, child, and congregation concerning the salvation of the children. This is supposed to be a powerful argument. "Who knows with certainty," they ask, triumphantly, "whether the infant presented for baptism by the godly couple is elect or reprobate?"

In fact, their argument is foolish. For, first, we do not know with absolute certainty the election and salvation even of the godly couple—the parents—who present their child for baptism. It is possible that one or both are hypocrites. We regard them also, sincerely, with the judgment of charity. This is our covenant judgment of the godly couple on the basis of their confession and walk. But only God and the godly couple themselves know with absolute certainty that the two who present the child for baptism are elect, saved children of God. Is there any Reformed church that has not had the painful experience that one whom they regarded as a godly man or a godly woman when he or she presented a child for baptism falls away and evidently perishes everlastingly? "They went out from us" (1 John 2:19).

In addition, despite all the loud trumpetings of the men of the federal vision that their doctrine gives absolute

4   Canons of Dordt, 1.17, in ibid., 3:585.

certainty concerning the salvation of every baptized infant, their affirmation of the salvation of every baptized child is meaningless, deceiving, heretical, and false. Their trumpetings are mere, loud noise. For, according to the theology of the federal vision, the child—*every* child—can lose his salvation and perish everlastingly. No more than the orthodox Reformed do the men of the federal vision know with certainty *the everlasting salvation* of any baptized child. And it is the intent of the question "Is a particular infant a covenant child?" to ask not about a temporary salvation that can be lost, but about the eternal salvation of the child.

Fourth, orthodox Reformed theologians in the past, including Ursinus, spoke of conditions in the covenant. They meant only that faith was the necessary means by which God accomplishes the salvation of the elect members of the covenant, as also the necessary means by which the elect receive and enjoy the benefits of the covenant. Even then, they themselves often noted that they were using "condition" in an "improper sense."

The proper sense of "condition" is an act required of someone upon which the act of another depends. It is in this grammatically proper, but theologically heretical, sense that the men of the federal vision speak of conditions in the covenant. Their teaching is that faith and obedience are works of baptized children upon which God's continued and everlasting salvation depend. In the theology of the federal vision, faith and obedience are works of the baptized children by which they distinguish themselves from other baptized children who have received the same covenant grace as themselves.

In view of the prevalent use of "condition" by the men of the federal vision, as by the Arminians and Roman Catholics before them, on behalf of heresy, Reformed theologians and church members who are zealous for the gospel of grace and opposed to the false gospel of salvation's depending on the will and works of the sinner will avoid speaking of conditions. They will describe faith as the necessary means of covenant salvation—*and the gracious gift of God.*

THE FEDERAL VISION
AND ITS CONSEQUENCES 13

Where do the men of the federal vision find their comfort in this life and for the life to come?

The theology of the federal vision is a doctrine of terror for those who believe it. The theologians of the federal vision would say that their teaching does not terrify them, because they are confident that they will perform the conditions upon which their salvation depends. Depending on their own ability to perform the conditions of salvation (always with the *help* of grace, but never by *irresistible* grace), they lean on a broken reed. They *admit* it. Their doctrine teaches that every one who is united to Christ, every believer, including the leading lights of the federal vision, can possibly lose his faith and salvation and perish everlastingly. This is terror. This is the ultimate terror.

It was a main purpose of the sixteenth-century Reformation of the church to deliver the people of God from this terror. Rome taught then, and still teaches today, that all believers must live in the fear of falling away into perdition. No one may be assured of final salvation, except perhaps a few who receive a special revelation. From this fear, the Reformation delivered all elect believers, weak ones as well as strong ones.

The Heidelberg Catechism expresses the assurance of salvation of every believing child of God, which the gospel of the Reformation restored to the people of God: "What is thy only comfort in life and in death? That I...belong to my faithful Saviour Jesus Christ...He also assures me of eternal life."[1] No Roman Catholic has this comfort. No Arminian has this comfort. Neither does any adherent of the federal vision.

If God begins a good work in us, he will "perform it until the day of Jesus Christ" (Phil. 1:6).

If I have faith, no matter how weak, if I believe the gospel of grace from the heart, I am sure of my final salvation. The reason is not that I am sure that I will perform conditions upon which this final salvation depends. Of this I am not sure at all. But I am sure that God will perfect what he has begun in me. I am sure that God is faithful.

The Reformed faith is a gospel of fearlessness.

The federal vision is a religion of terror.

And this is a reason we oppose the federal vision.

What did you mean when you called the federal vision "a sword of Damocles"?

In the lecture I mentioned the sword of Damocles with regard to the teaching of the federal vision that, although all children at baptism are objects of the grace of God, are united to Christ, and receive the blessings of covenant salvation, they forever live in the peril of falling away from Christ, losing grace, and going to hell, by failing to perform the conditions of the covenant.

Regarding this wicked doctrine of the falling away of (covenant) saints, particularly covenant children, I said, "The federal vision is not embarrassed by this doctrine, but seemingly glories in it. The men of the federal vision emphasize it as one of their most important teachings. They call Reformed churches and parents to warn their children of this sword of Damocles hanging over their heads until the moment of their death, as though this dreadful threat will scare the children into living godly lives."

In Roman legend (recounted by Cicero) Damocles, a flatterer of the wealthy, powerful tyrant Dionysius II, remarked to the tyrant how fortunate the tyrant was. To show Damocles how dangerous the life of a ruler is, Dionysius had Damocles sit

---

1   Heidelberg Catechism, Q&A 1, in *Creeds of Christendom*, 3:307–08.

on his throne, surrounded by luxuries. But over Damocles' head hung a heavy, sharp sword suspended by only one hair of a horse's tail. Terrified, the sycophant at once begged to be allowed to vacate the position.

The federal vision, like the conditional theology it is developing, hangs the Damoclesian sword of the very real possibility of falling away from Christ and salvation into hell over the heads not only of the covenant children, but also of every one of us. The thin horse hair by which this sword is suspended over us is our own works. This threat, in comparison with which the sword of Damocles was small beer, is supposed to motivate us to live godly lives.

Do you see the federal vision as the developing of a form of "Christianity" palatable to a world steeped in pagan tenets, to attain a salvation of self through ritual and works? May this play a role in the development of antichrist?

I have no doubt that the vast majority of Reformed people, including those who express some dissatisfaction with the federal vision, would reject this question out of hand as the expression of extremism, perhaps absurdity.

The vast majority of Reformed people would be mistaken.

The theology of the federal vision is an astounding, unmistakable, significant stage in the great apostasy forecast for the last days in 2 Thessalonians 2:3: "That day [the day of the coming of Jesus Christ] shall not come, except there come a falling away [*apostasia*] first." This apostasy will prepare for antichrist: "And that man of sin be revealed, the son of perdition." The federal vision is a stage in the falling away (apostasy) at the very heart of the visible church of the twenty-first century— conservative Reformed, Presbyterian, and evangelical churches in North America and across the world.

My reasons for this judgment upon the federal vision are the following.

The federal vision denies justification by faith alone, teaching justification by faith and works. This is the fundamental issue between genuine Protestantism and the Roman Catholic

Church, as Luther, Calvin, and the entire sixteenth-century Reformation of the church contended, and as all the Reformed churches have acknowledged until recently. One with Rome in the fundamental heresy of righteousness and, therefore, salvation by works, the whole of the federal vision, theologians and people, has no power to resist the allure of Rome. It is not unlikely that it has no *interest* in resisting Rome.

Large numbers of Presbyterians, members of supposedly conservative Presbyterian churches, have already converted to Rome (or to the Eastern Orthodox Church, which can easily unite with Rome when Satan decides the time is ripe) because these Presbyterians embraced the theology of the federal vision. I have named one of these Presbyterians, who now is a leading apologist for Rome to other Presbyterians, in my book *The Covenant of God and the Children of Believers*.[2] This apostate has publicly declared that Norman Shepherd and his doctrine of justification by works played an important part in his falling away to the Roman Catholic Church.[3]

The Roman Catholic Church will play the leading role in the false religious body that serves the political antichrist—the beast from the earth of Revelation 13 and the false prophet of Revelation 19.

Not only does the federal vision deny justification by faith alone, but it also denies all the doctrines of grace as confessed by the Canons of Dordt, from eternal predestination as the source of all grace, blessing, and salvation to the perseverance of the saints. Denying these grand truths of the gospel of grace, the federal vision shows itself to be essentially one with Arminianism, which is, in principle, modernism, and invariably leads to open modernism. Theological modernism is antichristian and works aggressively for the coming of antichrist.

In the language of Romans 9:16, by denying the true gospel, that salvation is of God who shows mercy, the federal vision

2 Engelsma, *Covenant of God*, 169–170.

3 Scott and Kimberly Hahn, *Rome Sweet Home: Our Journey to Catholicism* (San Francisco: Ignatius Press, 1993), 31.

confesses the false gospel, that salvation is of him who wills and runs (works). The false gospel serves antichrist, specifically by promoting the great falling away.

Then there is this hard fact that the federal vision is part of a much bigger theological movement among many of the hitherto conservative Reformed, Presbyterian, and evangelical bodies. This movement is deliberately rejecting the theology of the Reformation—the gospel of salvation by sovereign grace alone—particularly as this theology is embodied in the Reformed creeds, especially the Canons of Dordt and the Westminster standards. (The movement also is in the process of a radical revising of the orthodox doctrine of Scripture, but this is another, related story.) This movement does not as yet always and everywhere make its position as clear as does the federal vision. It is shrewd as Beelzebub. But the movement is a reality, and it is far advanced in institutions that many of the members of the churches still regard as bastions of orthodoxy. It is bent on the overthrow of the historic Reformed faith. The alternative, call it what they will, is the Arminian theology of free will, or some kind of universalism.

Those who teach and believe this doctrine will easily return to Rome. Their justification for their reunion with Rome will be twofold: ecumenicity and helping Rome fight the culture wars, thus establishing a carnal kingdom of Christ in history.

What is widely overlooked concerning the federal vision, and ought not be overlooked, is that it is avowedly and enthusiastically postmillennial, committed to "Christianizing" the culture of North America and eventually of the world. Most of the men of the federal vision are Christian reconstructionists.

Code words and code phrases that indicate the working of this broader movement to discredit and abandon the theology of the Reformation—the gospel of grace—in the conservative churches include "scholastic" and "systematic theology," with (veiled) contemptuous reference to the Canons of Dordt and the Westminster standards. The movement pleads for "biblical theology," as though the Canons and Westminster are unbiblical, indeed antibiblical. Invariably, the fruit of this biblical theology is the repudiation of eternal, unconditional, discriminating election as the source of Jesus Christ, of the gospel, of grace, of the covenant, and of salvation.

One obvious connection of the federal vision to the bigger movement I am referring to is the close ties of the federal vision with the new perspective on Paul, particularly as persuasively taught by the Anglican clergyman N. T. Wright. He makes no secret of the fact that one of the main purposes of his theology, if not the main purpose, is fellowship of evangelicals, Reformed, and Presbyterians with Roman Catholics at the Lord's supper, that is, at the Roman Catholic mass. Protestants, whom Wright is successfully wooing, will have this fellowship by joining the Roman Catholic Church.

I witnessed the extraordinary popularity and influence of Wright. A few years ago, Calvin Theological Seminary in Grand Rapids, Michigan, the seminary of the Christian Reformed Church, sponsored an all-day conference of theologians at which N. T. Wright was the teacher. More than three hundred theologians and ministers from all over North America, including representatives from virtually every reputedly conservative Reformed, Presbyterian, and evangelical seminary, attended.

Wright's subject was the book of Romans.

He began by saying that his purpose was to encourage "table fellowship" of conservative evangelicals and Roman Catholics. This means communal celebration of the sacrament of the Lord's supper. This means that evangelicals partake of the Roman Catholic mass. And this means that evangelicals join the Roman Catholic Church.

In several sessions Wright took the audience through the book of Romans, exercising his vaunted exegetical skills on the book. Such were these skills that they enabled him to deny, *in the book of Romans*, every cardinal doctrine of the Reformed faith as set forth in the confessions, from justification by faith alone to eternal, unconditional predestination.

At the end of the day, the nearly four hundred, mostly conservative, Reformed, Presbyterian, or evangelical theologians stood to give Wright a rousing, lasting ovation. Only a handful did not join in. They were praying, or should have been praying, "God have mercy on the members of Reformed churches today."

The federal vision is essentially Roman Catholic theology—justification by works, salvation by the will and works of men and women performing the conditions of the covenant, and baptismal covenant union with Christ (Rome calls it regeneration). The federal vision leads to the Roman Catholic Church.

Rome can make peace with the pagan religions (the question is whether the federal vision makes Christianity palatable to paganism). She has. She does. And she will. Pagan religions recognize the pomp, ceremony, and rituals of Rome, as well as the many saints worshiped by Roman Catholics. Pagan religions are thoroughly familiar with, and agreeable to, Rome's teaching of salvation by working.

THE FEDERAL VISION AND THE CHURCHES 14

I treat together several closely related questions. Are we to see the churches that embrace the federal vision as the false church? If not, how are we to view them? How are we to view the churches that fail to address the root of the federal vision and declare peace and health to their members? You say that the federal vision is one teaching among others that "brings the teaching of Arminianism up out of hell." How can those who belong to the Protestant Reformed Churches (and believe this statement) prove that this does not mean that God has not saved any of those who go to a church that openly teaches Arminianism? The charge has often been made against the Protestant Reformed Churches that except people repent of these heresies (federal vision, well-meant offer, etc.) they will go to hell in the judgment day. They cannot remain in their current denominations if they truly repent. Conclusion: only those who are Protestant Reformed can go to heaven. (This was done in a joking way already years ago when I attended Calvin College.)

This is what I said in the lecture about bringing out of hell again the Arminian heresy.

"What the United Reformed Churches' synod of 2010 ought to have decided is this. 'With regard to its doctrine of justification by faith and works and with regard to its denial of all the doctrines of salvation by sovereign grace in the covenant, synod declares the federal vision a heresy and advises every consistory vigorously to expose and condemn the federal vision, so that every member of the United Reformed Churches, man, woman, and child, is protected against this God-dishonoring and soul-destroying bringing up again of Arminianism out of hell.' And then the synod of the United Reformed Churches ought to have added: 'branch and root!' That is, 'Synod declares the federal vision heretical in its root, as well as in its fruit.'"

I borrowed the phrase "bringing up again of Arminianism out of hell" from the Canons of Dordt, which charge that Arminian theology "bring[s] again out of hell the Pelagian error."[1] Arminianism, therefore, according to the considered, official judgment of the Reformed faith and of true Reformed churches, is itself a doctrine out of hell—a more subtle form of Pelagianism. The theology of the federal vision (I demonstrated in my lecture and in other writings) is, in regard to the truths of predestination, of the death of Christ, of irresistible grace, and of the perseverance of the saints, the Arminian heresy of a (saving) grace of God in Christ that is wider than the election of a certain number, conditional, resistible, and losable.

In addition, the theology of the federal vision openly teaches the semi-Pelagian, Roman Catholic doctrine of justification by faith and works.

The federal vision is a form of the Arminian and Pelagian doctrine, the origin of which is hell.

In my lecture, I was mainly concerned to judge the *doctrine* of the federal vision—not men and not churches. My calling is to judge doctrines.

But of course (as some of these questions recognize), the fact that the federal vision is gross heresy, the source of which is Satan, who according to our Lord is the father of the lie (John 8:44), has implications for specific denominations of churches that either have officially approved the federal vision or are tolerating it. The implication for those churches that have officially approved the heresy of the federal vision is that they now plainly display the marks of the false church. They

---

1   Canons of Dordt, 2, Rejection of Errors 3, in *Confessions and Church Order*, 165.

have corrupted the preaching of the pure doctrine of the gospel at its very heart—justification by faith alone and all the related doctrines of salvation by grace alone. They have allowed at the table of the Lord heretics who preach and teach false doctrine. They have refused to exercise Christian discipline upon men who show themselves unbelieving by teaching false doctrine.

Churches that tolerate the theology of the federal vision and protect its proponents are little less culpable. They are merely shrewder. They refuse to condemn the heresy, because that would cause trouble and division. They may lose members. Or their heart is really with the conditional covenant theology of the federal vision.

Some churches refrain from openly approving the federal vision because they are concerned to keep a reputation of Reformed orthodoxy. The federal vision, after all, denies the fundamental doctrine of the sixteenth-century Reformation of the church. Eventually, these churches will come to an open approval of the false doctrine. Over the fundamental issues raised by the federal vision, no church can for long halt between the two opinions.

There are consequences for the members of these churches. When the Synod of Dordt rejected Arminianism as a doctrine out of hell—at huge cost, effort, struggle, and suffering—and when it defended the Reformation's (and the Bible's) gospel of particular, sovereign grace—in a controversy that convulsed the Netherlands and much of Europe—it did so *because it was convinced both that God is glorified only by the gospel of sovereign grace and that he saves his people by means of the gospel of sovereign grace.*

Those who believe and practice the lie of Arminianism as it takes form in the federal vision, that is, trust for their righteousness and salvation in their own works and worth—their performing of the conditions—and do not submit to the righteousness of God worked out in the lifelong obedience and in the death of Jesus Christ, go lost. And this takes place under the judgment of God, which falls upon a church that approves or tolerates the lie of salvation by the will or works of the sinner.

"[Salvation] is not of him that willeth, nor of him that runneth [works], but of God that sheweth mercy" (Rom. 9:16).

A church that takes on the marks of the false church by corrupting the gospel of grace does not all at once become wholly false. It embarks on a sure, steady, and often swift process of decline into the abyss. Those churches that now embrace the federal vision will eventually go back to the Roman Catholic Church. They are one in the fundamental doctrine: justification by faith and good works. Between Rome's teaching that the good works "merit" and the federal vision's teaching that the good works are causal conditions, there is no essential difference.

As for the members, the elect believers will be saved, contrary to the teaching of the men of the federal vision (who teach that elect believers can perish), although God will chastise them. But, remaining in the apostatizing churches, they will certainly go lost in their generations, and as we see today, this happens swiftly—often already in the first or second generation.

One thing our sentimental, tolerant, doctrinally indifferent Christian community needs to hear is that churches can and do become false. Churches that once were sound, and that still have a name for conservatism, can become false. There is a reason for the sharp warning of article 29 of the Belgic Confession regarding false churches and for the instruction of this article regarding what the marks of a church that has become false, or is becoming false, are. We are living in the last days. And the last days are marked by a great falling away. The Bible says so: "That day [the day of Christ] shall not come, except there come a falling away first" (2 Thess. 2:3).

I have carefully explained this matter of true and false churches in detail in my recent book *Bound to Join* and refer the interested reader to the book, especially for the account of a church's becoming false.[2]

The Protestant Reformed Churches and their spokesmen have never dreamed of teaching that only members of these

2   David J. Engelsma, *Bound to Join: Letters on Church Membership* (Jenison, MI: Reformed Free Publishing Association, 2010).

churches are saved. The charge that we teach this is a slander by those who cannot refute our defense of the gospel of grace and who are angered by our criticism of their corruption of the gospel of grace. Rather than address the issues, they revile the churches. It is the old story of killing the messenger.

We are far too busy working on behalf of our own membership's salvation, including working out our salvation in all areas of life in a wicked and hostile world, to wile away our time idly questioning the salvation of the members of other churches.

We hope God has multitudes of his saved people outside the Protestant Reformed Churches, in all the world. Wherever they are, they are, like us, justified by faith alone—apart from all works of their own; they are, like us, totally depraved sinners, who are saved by irresistible grace; they are, like us, infallibly preserved unto everlasting glory; they are, like us, saved only on the basis of the atoning death of Christ, which satisfied, then and there, at Golgotha some two thousand years ago, for every one for whom he died; and they are, like us, saved because God elected them unto grace and glory in the eternal, unconditional decree. And wherever they are, they, like us, give to God alone the glory of their salvation—not merely in the mouthing of a cliché, but in the content of their confession and by a godly life.

If God has at present kept only a few, as in the days of Noah (when the church numbered eight in a world of millions), or as in the time of Elijah (when he reserved to himself only seven thousand among the hundreds of thousands in Israel), our calling remains the same: hold the traditions (2 Thess. 2:15)!

One of these traditions is justification by faith alone, apart from good works, specifically the good works we do by the grace of the Holy Spirit.

The newness of this federal vision in our time makes it a danger. How do we deal with brothers who are misled?

By these answers to questions on the subject of the federal vision, by other writings, and by the warnings I give in preaching, I am dealing with brothers and sisters who may be misled or confused by this contemporary false doctrine in the Reformed churches.

Southwest Protestant Reformed Church's evangelism society and other Protestant Reformed churches exert themselves to be of assistance, by means of public lectures, especially to fellow Reformed Christians who may be struggling with the teachings of the federal vision. Southwest Protestant Reformed Church in Wyoming, Michigan, and the other Protestant Reformed churches that sponsor these lectures ought to be commended. The others are the Protestant Reformed churches in Hull, Iowa; Randolph, Wisconsin; and Crete, Illinois.

All Reformed believers who know and love the faith of the Heidelberg Catechism, the Belgic Confession, and the Canons of Dordt can discuss the issues raised by the men of the federal vision with brothers and sisters who are being misled or are simply ignorant of the fundamental truths now at stake in the Reformed community of churches, for example, justification by faith alone—the heart of the gospel. And this is the duty of every Reformed believer in the office of believer as a prophet or prophetess.

As we deal in these ways with brothers and sisters who are misled, we must make plain to them the seriousness of their being misled by the heresy. It is the same as the seriousness of the Galatians' being misled by the false teaching Paul condemns in the letter to the Galatians: "If ye be circumcised, Christ shall profit you nothing...Christ is become of no effect unto you, whosoever of you are justified by the law" (Gal. 5:2–4).

To those being deceived today by the federal vision, the apostle says, "If you depend for your righteousness before God today or in the final judgment upon one, single, puny good work of your own, Christ shall profit you nothing...Christ is become of no effect unto you, whosoever of you are justified by the law."

About the teachers of the theology of the federal vision, we say, in the presence of those who are misled, "I would they were even cut off which trouble you [Reformed people of God]" (v. 12).

Do the liberated Reformed Churches in the Netherlands (and their daughter churches, the Canadian Reformed Churches in North America and the Free Reformed Churches in Australia) teach that people in the covenant, united to Christ and saved, can fall away? That is, do the liberated churches agree with the federal vision? If not, could we not say that conditions in the theology of the liberated churches are also merely necessary means (in the sense that the Westminster Confession uses the word "conditions") whereby God saves his elect?

This question obviously has in view the remark I made in the lecture that the Westminster standards and orthodox theologians in the past spoke of faith as the condition of the covenant, meaning only that faith is the necessary means by which God establishes the covenant with his elect, by which he bestows the benefits of the covenant, and by which the covenant child of God receives and enjoys the benefits of the covenant. Even though it now becomes plain that the use of "condition" to express necessary means was a poor choice and dangerous (and some of the orthodox Reformed theologians in the past saw this and admitted that they were using "condition" in an "improper sense"), the doctrine itself was orthodox.

The question asks whether the Reformed Churches in the Netherlands (liberated) might not also use "condition" in their doctrine of the covenant in a good, orthodox sense. Or is the conditional covenant doctrine of the liberated churches the same as the heretical doctrine of the federal vision?

The theology of the federal vision is the development of the doctrine of the covenant of the Reformed Churches in the Netherlands (liberated), of the Canadian Reformed Churches, and of the Free Reformed Churches in Australia.

The federal vision openly declares that it is developing the doctrine of the covenant of Klaas Schilder and the liberated churches; the entire Reformed community in North America knows that the federal vision is the development of the covenant theology of the liberated churches (although the Reformed community bends over backward to avoid saying so); and the covenant doctrine itself of the federal vision shows, unmistakably, that it is the development of the doctrine of the liberated churches.

The doctrine of the covenant of the liberated churches (and its daughters in Canada and Australia) cuts the covenant loose from election. God's eternal election is not the source of the covenant. God's eternal election does not govern the covenant. Professor Cornelis Veenhof, one of the founding fathers of the liberated churches in the 1940s, informs us that he, Schilder, and others *deliberately decided* on a doctrine of the covenant that would cut the covenant loose from eternal election. "Very deliberately, what was taught concerning covenant, covenant promise, and baptism was *not* placed under the governing of election."[3]

So far did this go already in the earliest days of the liberated churches that another founding father and most influential theologian of those churches, Professor B. Holwerda, was publicly teaching that the only election found in the Bible, including Ephesians 1:4 and 2 Thessalonians 2:13, is a decision of God in time and history—an election dependent on conditions. Klaas Schilder knew this and did nothing about it.[4]

This is the covenant doctrine that the federal vision is developing.

Following from this denial of election, the liberated churches teach that the covenant, its blessings, and its salvation are conditional. The covenant depends on works that the children must perform. The works are faith and obedience. So much is this the teaching of the liberated churches that they *define* the covenant as "promise and demand." The covenant is God's promise to every child, "I will be your God and save you," and his demand of every child, "Believe in Christ and obey me." The demand is the condition that the child must perform. Upon this condition God's promise depends. If the child fails to perform

3 C. Veenhof, *Prediking en uitverkiezing* [Preaching and election] (Kampen: Kok, 1959), 299; my translation of the Dutch.

4 See the acknowledgment of this by a liberated theologian, Erik de Boer, "Unfinished Homework: Charting the Influence of B. Holwerda with Respect to the Doctrine of Election," trans. Nelson D. Kloosterman, *Mid-America Journal of Theology* 18 (2007): 107–36.

the condition, God retracts the promise that he once made to the child, and the covenant that God once established with the child is annulled. The child goes lost. The covenant, therefore, depends not on the promising God and thus on God's election, but on the child who performs the condition.

And this spells the radical difference between the use of "condition" in the Westminster Confession in an orthodox sense and the meaning of "condition" in the covenant theology of the liberated churches and in the covenant theology of the federal vision.

The Westminster Confession and some orthodox theologians in the past spoke of faith as the condition of the covenant. What they meant by condition was the necessary means by which God realizes his covenant promise with the elect.

The Westminster Confession and the orthodox theologians taught that election governs the covenant, covenant grace, and covenant salvation. The Westminster Larger Catechism expressly states that God made the covenant with Christ and with the elect: "With whom was the covenant of grace made? The covenant of grace was made with Christ as the second Adam, and in him with all the elect as his seed."[5]

When the Westminster standards then speak of faith as the condition, they do not mean that the covenant grace of God, which is supposed to be wider than election, depends on the faith and obedience of the child. They do not mean by condition a work of the child upon which God's covenant and its salvation depend, or a work by which some children distinguish themselves from other children, who like themselves are objects of the covenant grace of God. The Westminster standards mean by "condition" the necessary means by which God establishes his covenant with the elect children and the necessary means by which the elect children receive and enjoy the covenant blessing.

Radically different is the use of "condition" by the liberated churches. In the covenant theology of the liberated churches,

5 Westminster Larger Catechism, Q&A 31, in *Confession of Faith and Subordinate Standards*, 57.

God makes his covenant with all the children alike (for election does not control the covenant). Now, "condition" refers to *a work of the children upon which the covenant depends regarding its being maintained with the children, regarding its blessing of the children, and regarding its saving of the children.* Now, "condition" refers to *a work of the children by which the children distinguish themselves from other children (who are in the covenant as much as are the children who perform the conditions) regarding their salvation.*

The proper linguistic meaning of "condition" is that upon which something depends. The liberated churches teach a conditional covenant in this sense of the word "condition." They teach that the faith and the faithfulness of the baptized children are works of the children upon which the covenant of God with them depends.

Using "condition" in this way, the liberated churches are heretical in their theology of the covenant. They teach that the covenant, covenant blessings, and covenant salvation depend upon the children, who perform the conditions, rather than upon the promising God. This is the necessary, unavoidable implication of their cutting the covenant loose from election. Cutting the covenant loose from election means that the covenant does not depend on God.

The liberated theologians have attempted to deflect this charge by responding that "God fulfills the conditions." But the attempt is a failure in every respect.

First, it makes no difference that some children perform the conditions with the help of God. The fact remains that the covenant depends on the work of the children, rather than on the electing grace of God.

Second, the response, if it is seriously meant, contradicts the heart of the liberated covenant theology: Election does not govern the covenant. If God fulfills the conditions in some children, why does he do so only with some and not with the others? There are only two possible answers. One is that God has elected these children in distinction from the others, whom he has not elected but reprobated. The covenant depends on election after all. But the liberated repudiate this theology of the covenant. They detest it. Therefore, they are committed to the only other possible answer: Those children in whom God fulfills the conditions must show themselves worthy of this. Still, then, the covenant depends on the children.

The federal vision is a development of this doctrine of the covenant. The men of the federal vision are bringing out all the implications of the liberated doctrine of the covenant: justification by works; a death of Christ for all the children that fails to save many for whom Christ died; resistible grace; a falling away from Christ. These and more dreadful heresies, plainly opposed to the Reformed creeds, are all implicit in the liberated doctrine of the conditional covenant.

In the past liberated ministers would not admit that their covenant doctrine implied these heresies. In spite of the contradiction, they would confess the doctrines of Dordt along with their covenant theology. No doubt, they were sincere.

But their covenant doctrine taught that God is gracious to all the baptized children of godly parents alike. The covenant promise is gracious—and it comes to all alike! The covenant of God is gracious—and he makes it with all the children alike! The blessings spoken of in the Reformed baptism form are grace—and according to the liberated these blessings apply to all the baptized children alike!

The liberated, therefore, have always taught a covenant grace of God in Jesus Christ *for all baptized children*, which is conditional, resistible, and losable. The liberated have always taught the falling away from covenant grace of many children, even though the ministers and theologians were very cautious how they expressed it, knowing full well that they were treading on desperately dangerous ground.

The men of the federal vision are bold. They make explicit what always lay implicit in the covenant theology of the liberated churches: the denial of the sovereignty of God in predestination with regard to the covenant. No doubt they are carrying the covenant doctrine of the liberated churches further than some of the ministers in those churches like. But the covenant doctrine of the federal (covenant) vision is in all respects the faithful, logical, inevitable development of the covenant doctrine of the liberated churches.

That this is the case, the Canadian Reformed Churches acknowledge. (What the liberated churches in the Netherlands may make of the federal vision, I do not know; probably nothing—they have a host of other, equally grave matters on their agenda). The Canadian Reformed Churches not only refuse to condemn the federal vision, but also defend it at every opportunity. They welcome its most outspoken advocates as speakers at their seminary and ministers' gathering. When pressed (and it does press a Reformed church that a theology proclaims justification by works!), they will express vague unhappiness at some "extreme statements" on the part of "some" of the men of the federal vision.

The theologians of the Canadian Reformed Churches supported the federal vision from the very beginning. When Westminster Seminary in Philadelphia finally let Professor Norman Shepherd go, back in the early 1980s, Jelle Faber, at the time professor of dogmatics at the Canadian Reformed Seminary in Hamilton, Ontario, Canada, wrote an article angrily condemning the action of Westminster in letting Shepherd go and defending Shepherd's covenant theology (which had manifested itself by a denial of justification by faith alone and then by a seven-year defense of the denial of justification by faith alone).

The federal vision is the covenant doctrine of the liberated churches in more fully developed form.

The federal vision is the legitimate child of the liberated churches.

The child has grown up.

And he is a terror to the Reformed faith.

"God has begun his covenant, and its salvation, with you; from now on it is up to you."

This is terror.

The conditional covenant has been described as an extension of the theory of common grace into the covenant. Does the fact that there is no discussion of the federal vision in the Christian Reformed Church in North America indicate that the theology of the federal vision is taken for granted in the Christian Reformed Church?

The controversy over the federal vision is a battle for the distinctive truth of the Reformed faith within Presbyterian and Reformed churches that still take their official confession of the Reformed faith more or less seriously. There will never again be a battle for the Reformed faith in the Christian Reformed Church. The last battle in the Christian Reformed Church for the truth of salvation by the sovereign grace of God was the conflict over common grace, chiefly over the issue of a (saving) universal, resistible grace of God in the gospel of Jesus Christ (the well-meant offer), in 1924. Even the recent secession of some who then formed the United Reformed Churches was not a struggle over the Reformed faith. Christian Reformed people seceded because their church took a decision to allow women in ecclesiastical office. Women in ecclesiastical office is a tenet and practice of theological modernism.

The Christian Reformed Church in the twenty-first century has moved far beyond the issues that constitute the spiritual warfare of the Reformed faith with Arminianism or Amyrauldism. By this time it has fallen away into the depths of sheer modernism. It has put women into the special offices of the church; it produces and tolerates the open attack on the historicity of the first eleven chapters of the Bible and, thus, the denial that Scripture is the inspired word of God;[6] and it

---

6   Daniel C. Harlow, "After Adam: Reading Genesis in an Age of Evolutionary Science," *Perspectives in Science and Christian Faith* 62, no. 3 (September 2010): 179–95; John R. Schneider, "Recent Genetic Science and Christian Theology on Human Origins: An 'Aesthetic Supralapsarianism,'" *Perspectives in Science and Christian Faith* 62, no. 3 (September 2010): 196–212. Both Harlow and Schneider were professors at the Christian Reformed college, Calvin College, when they wrote these articles.

approves universalism—the teaching that in the end all humans will be saved.

Concerning the Christian Reformed Church's tacit or express approval of universalism in various stages of the modernist heresy, a synod of the Christian Reformed Church refused to condemn the teaching of universal atonement by a seminary professor, Harold Dekker, in the 1960s.[7] In the 1980s and 1990s Christian Reformed synods upheld the denial of reprobation and the affirmation of the possibility of universal salvation by Harry Boer.[8] Recently, a Christian Reformed synod rejected a protest against the bold promotion of universalism by Leonard Vander Zee.[9]

The Christian Reformed Church is in the process of publicly recognizing (and advertising) its abandonment of the Reformed faith by gutting the Formula of Subscription, which binds office-bearers (and thus the entire denomination) to the Reformed creeds.

Driving this falling away from the Reformed faith and life, that is, from Christ, has been the doctrine of common grace adopted by the Christian Reformed Church in 1924. The first point of the doctrine committed the Christian Reformed Church to a universal, saving love and grace of God in the gospel of Jesus Christ. All three points of their doctrine of common grace fatally breached the antithesis between the holy church and the unholy world, opening up that church to the world's thinking and doing.

This by no means implies that the Christian Reformed Church has no responsibility for the theology of the federal

7   Professor Dekker contended for universal atonement in a series of articles in the now-defunct magazine the *Reformed Journal*. The series included seven full-length articles and an important answer to a letter. The series and the answer to a letter ran in the *Reformed Journal* from December 1962 through September 1964. For the list of the articles and a brief analysis of the series, see David J. Engelsma, *Hyper-Calvinism and the Call of the Gospel* (Grand Rapids. MI: Reformed Free Publishing Association, rev. ed. 1994), 95–97.

8   Harry R. Boer, *The Doctrine of Reprobation in the Christian Reformed Church* (Grand Rapids, MI: Eerdmans, 1983); *An Ember Still Glowing: Humankind as the Image of God* (Grand Rapids, MI: Eerdmans, 1990).

9   Leonard J. Vander Zee, *Christ, Baptism and the Lord's Supper* (Downer's Grove, IL: InterVarsity, 2004).

vision in North America. Definitely contributing to the forming of the covenant theology of the federal vision in the broader Reformed community was the influential teaching in the Christian Reformed seminary for many years of William Heyns. He taught a gracious, conditional covenant of God with all the physical children of believers, involving a bestowal of grace upon all the children, which grace enables all to perform the condition of faith, if only they will. His covenant doctrine was essentially that out of which the federal vision has come and which the federal vision has developed.

Also, when in the early 1980s some heat was applied to Professor Norman Shepherd, contemporary father of the federal vision and of the controversy over that heresy, he left the Orthodox Presbyterian Church for the Christian Reformed Church, where he and his covenant theology are welcomed, perfectly at home, and protected from any possibility of discipline.

The Presbyterian churches do not see the root of the federal vision. Has the Lord shut their eyes? Is this a result of weak preaching in these churches?

It may well be that the doctrine of the covenant has been more thoroughly developed by and that it is more highly regarded in the Reformed churches of the Dutch tradition than anywhere else. This places a heavy responsibility upon these churches. God has given them this glorious aspect of his truth. They are called to maintain it purely, to develop its riches, and to live it. It is also their duty to defend the truth of the covenant when it is under attack, as is the case today in the controversy with the federal vision. God may be pleased to use this defense for the benefit of other churches where the doctrine of the covenant is not so central or so well developed.

Alas, also Reformed churches in the Dutch tradition fail, or refuse, to see the root of the federal vision.

Indeed, the root has sprung out of the Dutch Reformed tradition—out of bad soil in this tradition.

But there is another reason Presbyterian churches are handicapped in seeing clearly and repudiating the root of the federal vision. The Presbyterian creeds—the Westminster standards—use "condition" in connection with the covenant, as the three forms of unity never do. Question and answer 32 of the Larger Catechism reads in part: "How is the grace of God manifested in the second covenant? The grace of God is manifested in the second covenant, in that he freely provideth and offereth to sinners a Mediator, and life and salvation by him; and requiring faith as the condition to interest them in him."[10]

The Larger Catechism means by "condition" only that faith is the means of receiving the mediator of the covenant and his benefits. This is plain from the phrase that follows the word "condition" as virtually the definition of it: "to interest them in him." In addition, later the Catechism says especially about faith that it is "the way which he hath appointed them [the elect] to salvation."[11]

The Larger Catechism does not mean by "condition" a work of the sinner upon which covenant salvation is based and a work of the sinner by which he distinguishes himself from other sinners who are likewise objects and beneficiaries of covenant grace. That the Catechism does not mean this is evident from what the Catechism immediately adds: "[God] promiseth and giveth his Holy Spirit to all his elect, to work in them that faith, with all other saving graces."[12]

Nevertheless, when Presbyterian theologians promote the conditional covenant doctrine of the federal vision, of the liberated Reformed, and of others, they have a foothold among Presbyterians by virtue of the fact that the word "condition" has floated freely among Presbyterians in connection with the covenant.

Reformed people reared on the three forms of unity, in contrast, have an innate and deeply rooted suspicion of the word "condition" in connection with the covenant.

10   Westminster Larger Catechism, Q&A 32, in *Confession of Faith and Subordinate Standards*, 57.

11   Westminster Larger Catechism, A. 32, in ibid.

12   Westminster Larger Catechism, A. 32, in ibid.

THE FEDERAL VISION AND THE PROTESTANT REFORMED CHURCHES 15

In light of the current controversy over the covenant doctrine of the federal vision in almost all the Reformed and Presbyterian churches in North America, why is there no interest in those churches in the struggle of the Protestant Reformed Churches against the doctrine of a conditional covenant in the early 1950s? Why the silence on the part of the theologians concerning the struggle over the conditional covenant on the part of the Protestant Reformed Churches?

This question I cannot answer. I have no doubt that Reformed and Presbyterian theologians who are busying themselves today with the matter of the federal vision (and the controversy is forced upon them, because the theology of the federal vision is in their churches and is causing division) are well aware of the history of the struggle in the Protestant Reformed Churches in the late 1940s and early 1950s. They are all learned men. I could demonstrate, if I had a mind to, that some of them use arguments they have borrowed from Protestant Reformed writers. But they studiously avoid referring to the Protestant Reformed Churches. They never acknowledge the defense of Reformed orthodoxy concerning the covenant against the federal vision by Protestant Reformed ministers.

Why this is I do not know.

Nor care.

Except for one thing. Their ignoring of the history and of the covenant theology of the Protestant Reformed Churches goes hand in hand with their failure, or refusal, to take hold of the federal vision *at its root.* Therefore, the Protestant Reformed Churches speak out, and are called by God to speak out, about the federal vision.

One thing is sure. In his guidance of the history of the church and his development of the truth, the Spirit of Christ now confronts the entire conservative Reformed community of churches with essentially the same doctrinal issue over which the Protestant Reformed Churches struggled in a heart-wrenching and church-splitting way some sixty years ago. The only difference is the *development* of the doctrine of a conditional covenant by the men of the federal vision. The history of the Protestant Reformed Churches and the covenant theology of these churches could be of help to those churches and theologians who are serious about defending the gospel of sovereign grace with regard to the covenant.

Has the synod of the Protestant Reformed Churches made any official statements concerning the federal vision? If so, where can these statements be found?

The synod of the Protestant Reformed Churches has made no official statement concerning the federal vision. It has not had to make a statement. No professor, minister, or elder has taught the doctrines of the federal vision, expressed any sympathy for those heresies, or indicated any openness to them. A powerful reason for this, in the special providence of God, is that in the early 1950s the Protestant Reformed Churches repudiated the doctrine that is at the root of the federal vision, namely, the doctrine of a conditional covenant as taught by Klaas Schilder, Benne Holwerda, Cornelis Veenhof, and other theologians of the Reformed Churches in the Netherlands (liberated).

As I said in my lecture, the advocates of the federal vision "advertise their theology as the covenant doctrine of Schilder and the liberated churches." The critics of the federal vision recognize that the federal vision is the development of the covenant doctrine of Schilder and the liberated churches. At the

Knox Colloquium in 2003, Carl Robbins, one of the critics of the federal vision, announced to the gathering:

> I've finally grasped that he [John Barach, as spokesman for the federal vision] is simply re-stating the distinctive [covenant theology] of the 'Liberated' Reformed Churches. Therefore, it must fairly be pointed out that Pastor Barach cannot be charged with 'theological novelty,' for his views were first propounded by Klaas Schilder in the 1940s and (before him) Calvin Seminary Professor William W. Heyns from the early 1900s. In fact, Pastor Barach has simply and faithfully re-stated those covenantal understandings.[1]

The 1951 synod of the Protestant Reformed Churches adopted a document demonstrating that the Reformed confessions condemn the doctrine of a conditional covenant with all the baptized children of godly parents alike and expressing that the Protestant Reformed Churches confess the unconditional covenant of grace with the elect only. This document is the Declaration of Principles of the Protestant Reformed Churches.[2]

About this document, I said in the lecture that it "ought to be the most sought after and highly prized document in the community of Reformed and Presbyterian churches in North America...It is *the* manual for detecting and eradicating the root of the heresy in the Reformed churches that is the federal vision."

Why do federal vision advocates Steve Schlissel and Peter Leithart frequently refer to Herman Hoeksema, along with Klaas Schilder and Abraham Kuyper, to justify their view of the covenant?

The advocates of the federal vision sometimes appeal to Herman Hoeksema in support of two aspects of their doctrine

---

1 Robbins, "A Response to 'Covenant and Election,'" in *Auburn Avenue Theology*, 157.

2 The Declaration is found in *Confessions and Church Order*, 412–31. A copy of the Declaration can be obtained from the Reformed Free Publishing Association, the publisher of *Federal Vision: Heresy at the Root*.

of the covenant. One aspect is their view of the essence of the covenant as a relationship of communion in love, rather than as a contract or agreement. The other is their rejection of the covenant with Adam in paradise as a covenant of works in the sense that Adam could have merited a higher, better, heavenly, and eternal life by his work of not eating the forbidden fruit. In both of these aspects, their appeal to Herman Hoeksema is right. He saw the covenant as a living relationship of love and friendship, rooted ultimately in the love-life of the blessed Trinity. He did reject the traditional doctrine of the covenant with Adam as a covenant of works in the sense that Adam, by his obedience, could have merited the highest life possible for man, which Jesus Christ earned and obtained for the new human race by his incarnation, lifelong obedience, and especially his atoning death.

I appreciate the acknowledgment by the men of the federal vision that they are indebted to Herman Hoeksema for their understanding of the covenant as a bond of fellowship in love. This is honorable on their part. It is a shabby thing that many other Reformed theologians who have obviously changed their conception of the covenant from a contract, or bargain, to a bond of love under the influence of Hoeksema refuse to credit the great Protestant Reformed theologian.

But even with respect to these two aspects of the overall doctrine of the covenant, the agreement of the federal vision with Hoeksema is more apparent than real. The federal vision, for example, although denying that Adam could have *merited* the higher, eternal life, teaches that Adam might have *matured* into that life by faithful obedience. Here the men of the federal vision follow the bizarre, allegorical exegesis of James Jordan, who makes Harold Camping seem a sober exegete. Hoeksema denied that Adam could have taken the race into the higher, eternal life that Christ has now earned for us in any manner whatever, whether meriting or maturing. Only the eternal Son of God in our flesh, "the Lord from heaven" (1 Cor. 15:47), by his unique obedience, could give us "the image of the heavenly" (v. 49).

Regarding the fundamental aspect of their doctrine of the covenant, the root of all their heresies, namely, the doctrine of the conditional covenant, the federal vision emphatically does *not* appeal to Hoeksema. It has no such foe as he—and the Protestant Reformed Churches. No other critics are real adversaries, opposing the federal vision as the Arminian heresy *with regard to the covenant* and condemning it at its root— the doctrine of a gracious, conditional covenant with all the children of believers alike.

For the essence of their doctrine of the covenant, the men of the federal vision appeal to Klaas Schilder, and rightly so.

Why do members of the Protestant Reformed Churches need to be so concerned about the false teachings of the federal vision? It seems like we have heard a lot lately in many sermons and speeches about the false teachings of the federal vision. Is it because there is a big concern that members of the Protestant Reformed Churches will believe these false teachings? If not, why then is there so much talk about the federal vision?

I am greatly encouraged by this question. It indicates that the Protestant Reformed ministers are carrying out their calling from God to warn and instruct their congregations concerning one of the most serious threats to the Reformed faith, that is, to the gospel of grace; to the glory of God in that gospel; and to the souls of God's people, since the time of the Synod of Dordt. Not that I doubted that Protestant Reformed ministers are doing this.

Here are the reasons Protestant Reformed ministers and professors are giving, and are called by Christ himself to give, thorough instruction and sharp warning concerning the heresy of the federal vision.

First, every minister has vowed to God that he will defend the doctrine confessed in the three forms of unity against all attacks on it. He made this vow when he signed the Formula of Subscription. The federal vision is a bold attack on the theology (the doctrine of God) of the three forms of unity. In addition, every minister has promised that he will "refute and contradict" doctrines that militate against the doctrine of the three forms of unity and especially doctrines that militate against the doctrine taught in the Canons of Dordt. Indeed, he has promised that he is "disposed" to do this.[3] The federal vision has launched its attack on the Reformed faith of the creeds specifically against the truth of salvation by sovereign grace confessed by the Canons of Dordt. If a Protestant Reformed minister does not defend the truth of justification by faith alone and with it the five points of Calvinism against the assault on it and denial of it *within the conservative Reformed and Presbyterian churches*, he is unfaithful to his vow at his signing of the Formula of Subscription.

Also, the Reformed Church Order of Dordt, which is the church order of the Protestant Reformed Churches, as of many other Reformed denominations, states this about the calling of ministers and elders:

> To ward off false doctrines and errors that multiply exceedingly through heretical writings, the ministers and elders shall use the means of teaching, of refutation or warning, and of admonition, as well in the ministry of the Word as in Christian teaching and family-visiting.[4]

Faithful ministers and elders both in the Protestant Reformed Churches and elsewhere, who care for their congregations and who are concerned to give an account of their ministry to Christ at the end of the day, will warn against the federal vision, which is multiplying exceedingly through heretical writings.

This promise, to defend the faith and to warn the members of the Protestant Reformed Churches against attacks on it, is obedience to the charge of Ezekiel to officebearers that, as faithful watchmen, they warn the people of God when danger threatens (Ezek. 33 and 34).

---

3   Formula of Subscription, in ibid., 326.
4   Church Order of the Protestant Reformed Churches, Art. 55, in ibid., 397.

In the New Testament in virtually every epistle, the Holy Spirit points out the calling of ministers and ruling elders to expose and condemn false doctrines, so that the congregations and their members will not be led astray (Gal. 1; 2 Peter 2; 2 Tim. 2; and many other places). All these New Testament passages reflect the warning of Jesus in Matthew 24:4–5, in John 10:1–13, and in other places that the great danger to the church in the end times is deception by false teachers.

Second, it is the solemn duty particularly of the professor of theology that he "caution [the students] in regard to the errors and heresies of the old, but especially of the new day."[5] Certainly, one of the reasons for this is that the students, when they become ministers, can warn the people about the errors especially of the new day.

Article 18 of the Church Order of Dordt, which is the church order of the Protestant Reformed Churches, requires of professors of theology that they "expound the Holy Scriptures and...*vindicate sound doctrine against heresies and errors*."[6] If a professor of theology in a Reformed denomination bound by the Church Order of Dordt does not vindicate the sound doctrines of justification by faith alone, salvation by sovereign grace, and the covenant of grace against the heresies of the federal vision and of the new perspective on Paul, he is disobedient to article 18 of the church order and derelict in the exercise of his office as professor of theology.

Third, the heresy of the federal vision is the corruption of the fundamental truth of the gospel of grace, namely, that salvation is by grace alone, by Christ alone, to the glory of God alone. Basic to this truth is the heart of the gospel—justification by faith alone. It is exactly this grand truth that is challenged, denied, and subtly corrupted by the federal vision. *The Bible and church history make plain that it is always this truth that the devil works to destroy* (read Galatians and Romans; think

5   Form for the Installation of Professors of Theology, in ibid., 297.

6   Church Order of the Protestant Reformed Churches, Art. 18, in ibid., 386; emphasis added.

of the sixteenth-century Reformation of the church; remember the Synod of Dordt).

And the members of the Protestant Reformed Churches are not automatically immune to the threat. Not at all! Our sinful nature is as opposed to the truth of sovereign grace as was the nature of Jacob Arminius. I warn those who might be saying, "We would never fall for the federal vision," "Let him who thinks he stands take heed lest he fall."

The question seems to suggest that, because no federal vision proponent has appeared within the Protestant Reformed Churches, we can safely ignore the spreading attack on the gospel of grace. This is a mistake for several reasons. For one thing, Protestant Reformed people have many contacts—by means of friends, relatives, acquaintances in largely Reformed communities, teachers and fellow students in Reformed colleges, employers, employees, and more—with the churches in which the heresy of the federal vision has appeared, is promoted, is defended, or is tolerated. The Protestant Reformed denomination has recently sent observers to an ecumenical organization (NAPARC) in which Presbyterian and Reformed denominations are prominent and influential members that either have been responsible for the rise and spread of the federal vision, or have had very vocal advocates of the federal vision who have gone undisciplined, or today have professors, ministers, and ruling elders who teach and defend the federal vision or aggressively teach the doctrine of the covenant that is being developed by the federal vision, or all of these. I refer specifically to the Orthodox Presbyterian Church, the Presbyterian Church in America, the United Reformed Churches, and the Canadian and American Reformed Churches (liberated). These close contacts make it imperative that our people be instructed and warned concerning the federal vision—not desirable, but imperative.

For another thing, the federal vision spreads its heresy by writings—books, magazines, and the Internet. Protestant Reformed people read these writings and can be influenced by them. I mention one example: the books and other writings of the popular Douglas Wilson—one of the main leaders of the federal vision movement. Good instruction and sharp warning will keep people from being deceived and will enable them to give a defense of the truth against the error, which may help others. Fourth, good warning against the federal vision will also include careful explanation of the truth that is at stake. The contrast between the error and the truth will make the truth even clearer to our people. And growth in clear understanding of the truth is desirable. God always uses heresy for the clearer, richer understanding of the truth.

The God-given calling of Protestant Reformed ministers and professors to warn against the federal vision (and other false doctrines of our day) implies the God-given calling of Protestant Reformed people to sit for these warnings, to give themselves to the instruction and admonition of these warnings, and even to encourage the ministers and professors in carrying out their calling to give these warnings. Something would be seriously wrong in the churches if, when ministers and professors do what the churches require them to do in the Formula of Subscription, the Church Order, and the Form for the Installation of Professors of Theology (that is, what Christ himself requires the ministers to do), namely, warn the congregations concerning heresies and false teachings, the people refuse to hear the warnings, even do their best to avoid the warnings, criticize the faithful officebearers, and do all in their power to shut the professors' and ministers' mouths and shut down their word processors. Even such an unspiritual, disobedient response on the part of the people will not silence the ministers. For, as Ezekiel assures the faithful watchman in chapter 33 of his prophecy, by giving the warning the watchman is free of the blood of the people and their children.

But there is a fifth reason Protestant Reformed professors and ministers should be warning against the federal vision and giving good, thorough instruction concerning the great truths that are at stake in the controversy over the federal vision. That is the fact I pointed out in my lecture. Ministers and professors in no other denomination are addressing the root of the heresy of the federal vision. Some are rising to the defense of justification by faith alone. But this, serious as it is—the denial of the heart of the gospel—is not the root of the error. The root of the error is the doctrine of a conditional covenant of grace, established by God graciously with all the infants of godly parents alike, but dependent upon conditions that the infants must perform. Basic to this root of the heresy is the denial that God's eternal election of grace governs the covenant. I have demonstrated this many times and in many places, and need not do so again. *As long as this root remains in the Reformed and Presbyterian churches and seminaries, the federal vision will remain, flourish, and eventually conquer.* Only the Protestant Reformed Churches not only condemn all the bitter fruit, for example, the denial of justification by faith alone, but also get at the root of the evil—the heretical doctrine of a covenant of conditions.

At the same time we give witness to the truth of an unconditional covenant, that is, a covenant of grace—a covenant whose source and fountain is divine election and a covenant, therefore, that depends, from establishment to perfection, not upon conditions performed by the children, but upon the sovereign grace of God. Virtually alone among the churches in North America, the Protestant Reformed Churches testify to the unconditional covenant of grace—the positive side of its rejection of the doctrine of a conditional covenant.

Therefore, God gives to Protestant Reformed ministers and professors, as to all the people in these churches, a weighty and glorious calling: Defend the gospel of grace in its hour of crisis by taking hold of the grave threat to it at its root—as no other churches are doing! And at this crucial moment in church history, set forth the truth of the unconditional covenant!

We do this and must do this not only for our own sakes, but also for the sake of the Reformed faith in its truth and glory worldwide (regardless whether men hear or forebear—the effect of our testimony is God's business).

We must speak out, as evidently we alone are able and willing to do, for the good of Reformed churches worldwide, and in ages to come.

Suppose it is true, which it is not (have we so soon forgotten that sixty years ago two-thirds of the Protestant Reformed membership fell for the covenant doctrine that is the root of the federal vision, and split?)—suppose, I say, that there is no danger that Protestant Reformed people will be seduced by the federal vision. Have we no regard for our brothers and sisters in other Reformed churches? Have we no zeal for the faith itself that is being subverted? Have we no regard for the church of the future?

If we fall silent for any reason—discouragement that seemingly no one listens, a false notion of being loving, a desire to be accepted and approved by other churches, unwillingness to be hated for our confession of the truth of grace, or any other reason at all—God will raise up stones to make the confession we are privileged and called to make.

And I cannot see why we should have any pleasure in the prospect that our refusal to witness to the gospel of grace *in the matter of the covenant* becomes the occasion for God's turning to stones for a witness to the truth.

In light of the federal vision's denial of the active obedience of Christ, which is imputed to the believer, would you say that in the Protestant Reformed Churches there has not been enough emphasis on the distinction between the passive and active obedience of Christ?

Reformed theologians have proposed the distinction between the active obedience of Christ and the passive obedience of Christ. According to the distinction, Christ's passive obedience was his suffering and death in payment for sin. His active obedience was his perfect keeping of the law of God, not for himself, but on behalf of his people, especially to earn for them the right to eternal life. Both of these aspects of Christ's obedience are imputed to the believer, the passive obedience as taking away the guilt of sin and the active obedience as meriting eternal life, the passive obedience as satisfying the law's demand for punishment and the active obedience as satisfying the law's demand of a perfect keeping of its precepts.

The federal vision denies the imputation of the active obedience of Christ. According to the federal vision, Christ perfectly obeyed the law not as the substitute for his people, whose obedience is imputed to them, but only in order to be an acceptable sacrifice to God for the sins of the people. One who did not himself obey the law could not be the sacrifice for others.

Many men of the federal vision oppose imputation altogether: God's imputation of the guilt of sinners to Christ and his imputation of the obedience of Christ to sinners, whether the active obedience or the passive obedience. Thus they gut the Christian religion. One of the men of the federal vision, showing the mentality of the movement, has contemptuously dismissed imputation as God's doing "mental tricks or shuffling righteousness around heavenly ledgers."[7]

The distinction between the passive obedience and the active obedience of Christ leaves something to be desired. For in his passive obedience, that is, his suffering and dying, Jesus was intensely active. Indeed, he was never more active in obeying God than in his suffering and dying. He actively laid down his life. Actively, he loved God unto the death of the cross and in the worst agonies of that death. His sacrifice of himself—an action—was acceptable to God in the stead of the elect because Jesus actively offered himself to God in love.

Regarding the active obedience of Christ, therefore, which intends to refer to the obedience of Christ other than his suffering and death, in reality the active obedience of Christ was supremely his suffering and dying.

Nevertheless, the intent and doctrine of the distinction are correct. Not only was Christ the substitute for God's people in his suffering and dying, but he was also the substitute in his obedience to all the commands of the law. Not only is Christ our righteousness with regard to the satisfying of the law's demand

7 Lusk, "From Birmingham, With Love," in *A Faith That Is Never Alone*, 132.

upon guilty sinners that they be punished, but he is also our righteousness with regard to the satisfying of the law's demand that depraved sinners love God and the neighbor perfectly. Not only is there imputed to the believer in justification the sufferings and death of Christ with their benefits, but there is imputed also the lifelong obedience of Christ—his spotless holiness—with its benefits. The justified sinner stands before God, not only as one who has fully suffered the curse of the law—death and hell—that is due to guilt, but also as one who, "had never committed nor had any sin, and had myself accomplished all the obedience which Christ has fulfilled for me."[8]

The federal vision rejects the imputation of the active obedience of Christ. The reason is that for the federal vision (active) obedience to the law is something the believer must accomplish for himself. (Active) obedience to the law is the condition of the covenant, not part of the gift of righteousness in imputation. In addition, in the thinking of the men of the federal vision, to teach that a man—the believer—already possesses perfect fulfillment of all the commands of the law by imputation, through faith alone, would result in his becoming lazy in the Christian life, if not downright careless and profane. The thinking of the men of the federal vision is, "If I stand before God as one who has perfectly obeyed all the law, why should I exert myself to love God and the neighbor?"

The federal vision's denial of the imputation of the active obedience of Christ is part and parcel of its doctrine of a conditional covenant. Its error in this regard too, therefore, cannot successfully be refuted without taking hold of the root of the error: the rejection of the unconditional covenant (of grace).

The Reformed confessions teach the imputation of what Reformed theology has called the active obedience of Christ. The Heidelberg Catechism asserts that in justification there is imputed to the believer "the perfect satisfaction, righteousness, and holiness of Christ." The Catechism then makes plain that what is imputed is more than only the suffering and death of

8 Heidelberg Catechism, A. 60, in *Creeds of Christendom*, 3:326–27.

Christ, by adding that the benefit of justification is not only that the state of the believer is "as if I had never committed nor had any sin," but also that his state as justified is "as if I... had myself accomplished all the obedience which Christ has fulfilled for me."[9]

Answer 61 of the Heidelberg Catechism teaches the same: "The satisfaction, righteousness, and holiness of Christ is my righteousness before God."[10] Christ's holiness is all of his perfect life of love for God, not only his suffering and dying.

According to answer 115 of the Heidelberg Catechism, the believer learns from the strict preaching of the ten commandments to seek "forgiveness of sins and righteousness in Christ." "Righteousness" is here clearly distinguished from "forgiveness of sins" as Christ's fulfillment of all the demands of the law, which becomes the believer's by imputation through faith alone.[11]

Article 22 of the Belgic Confession states that Jesus Christ imputes to us "all his merits, and so many holy works, which he hath done for us and in our stead."[12] "So many holy works" include more than his holy work of dying. They are all his obedience to the will of God—his active obedience.

Although Scripture certainly emphasizes the suffering and death of Jesus Christ as the righteousness of the believer by imputation, it teaches also that the entire life of Jesus Christ was a life of willing subjection to the law of God not for himself, but for his people as the obedience to the law required of them, which becomes theirs by imputation. Christ was "made under the law, To redeem them that were under the law" (Gal. 4:4–5). His entire life, culminating in the cross, is the "obedience" of the one who constitutes many righteous by imputation (Rom. 5:19). Christ himself, the entire Christ in the whole of his work, not only a certain aspect of his work, is our righteousness by imputation.

9   Heidelberg Catechism, A. 60, in ibid.
10   Heidelberg Catechism, A. 61, in ibid., 3:327.
11   Heidelberg Catechism, A. 115, in ibid., 3:349.
12   Belgic Confession, Art. 22, in ibid., 3:408.

The issue is this. God's law demands perfect obedience of us. It not only demands that we be punished for our disobedience; it also demands obedience—a perfect love of God and a perfect love of the neighbor. Such is the teaching of the Heidelberg Catechism:

> What does the Law of God require of us?
>
> This Christ teaches us in sum, Matthew 22: *Thou shalt love the Lord thy God with all thy heart, and with all thy soul, and with all thy mind, and with all thy strength. This is the first and great commandment; and the second is like unto it: Thou shalt love thy neighbor as thyself.—On these two commandments hang all the law and the prophets.*[13]

We are unable to fulfill this demand. "Canst thou keep all this perfectly? No; for I am by nature prone to hate God and my neighbor."[14] "Even the holiest men, while in this life, have only a small beginning of this obedience."[15] If Christ did not obey in our place, so that now he may impute this obedience to us by faith alone, either all humans must be condemned—in which case God fails to save his chosen people and is both a liar and impotent—or God must waive his demand of perfect obedience, in which case he denies himself and is unjust.

The men of the federal vision may make their choice of these two options.

The question is: Have the Protestant Reformed Churches emphasized sufficiently the active obedience of Christ?

Perhaps not.

Perhaps even the creeds have not done full justice to the active obedience of Christ, although they certainly teach it.

God uses heresy to cause his church to come to a clearer and fuller knowledge of the truth. He is using the federal vision to do this especially with regard to the doctrine of the covenant, which

---

13 Heidelberg Catechism, Q&A 4, in ibid., 3:308–09.

14 Heidelberg Catechism, Q&A 5, in ibid., 3:309.

15 Heidelberg Catechism, A. 114, in ibid., 3:349.

is the root and the heart of that theology. But he uses the federal vision for the development also of the truth of justification.

Well may the Protestant Reformed Churches and other true churches of Christ respond to the federal vision not only by condemning its repudiation of the active obedience of Christ as part of the righteousness of justification, but also by searching more diligently into, and proclaiming more emphatically, this aspect of imputed righteousness.

The distinctive Protestant Reformed doctrine of the unbreakable bond of marriage was developed in direct relation to the doctrine of an unconditional covenant. If the Protestant Reformed Churches were to change their position on divorce and remarriage, would they ipso facto open themselves up to conditional theology? If so, why? If not, why not?

The day the Protestant Reformed Churches should change their stand regarding the unbreakable bond of marriage and allow for remarriage after divorce, they would also, in fact, be surrendering the truth of the unbreakable and unconditional covenant of grace. It would take a few years for this to work itself out, but work itself out it would.

My reason for this assertion is that the Bible establishes this close relation between marriage and the covenant. God has instituted marriage to be the picture, the earthly symbol, of his unbreakable covenant with the church. In Ezekiel 16, God calls his own covenant with Israel a marriage. Ezekiel 16 also teaches that, although Israel was unfaithful, and although God put her away for a while, he never broke the marriage bond, but renews it and takes Israel back in Jesus Christ. The church of Jews and Gentiles is the fulfillment of the reality of Israel, and the new covenant in Christ is the realization and renewal of the old covenant with Israel.

In the New Testament, Paul similarly relates covenant and marriage. In Ephesians 5, the apostle makes an extended comparison between earthly marriage and the covenant. Just as God's covenant with us is unbreakable, even when we commit spiritual adultery, so the earthly bond of marriage is an unbreakable bond for life.

That marriage is an unconditionally unbreakable bond for life, symbolizing the unconditional and, therefore, everlasting covenant of God with Christ and the elect, is the teaching of Scripture in many places. Among these is 1 Corinthians 7:39: "The wife is bound by the law as long as her husband liveth; but if her husband be dead, she is at liberty to be married to whom she will; only in the Lord."

The spiritual and theological mentality of conditionality and, therefore, dissolubility pervades and corrodes all relationships, human and divine. It is not the mind of God.[16]

16 For the doctrine of marriage that is confessed, preached, and practiced by the Protestant Reformed Churches, still at the beginning of the adulterous twenty-first century, see Herman Hoeksema, "The Covenant of Marriage" and "Divorce and Remarriage," in his *The Triple Knowledge: An Exposition of the Heidelberg Catechism*, vol. 3, 2nd ed. (Grand Rapids, MI: Reformed Free Publishing Association, 1976), 342–67; and David J. Engelsma, *Marriage, the Mystery of Christ and the Church: The Covenant-Bond in Scripture and History*, rev. ed. (Grandville, MI: Reformed Free Publishing Association, 1998).

THE FEDERAL VISION AND DEFENSE OF THE FAITH 16

If the merits of Christ's righteousness are the basis of our salvation, isn't preaching Christ and his righteousness a better response to the federal vision than getting bogged down in the intricacies of theological polemics?

Ah, yes, belittle and bedevil contending for the faith as "getting bogged down in the intricacies of theological polemics."

By the intricacies of theological polemics was the gospel of grace preserved against Arius.

By the intricacies of theological polemics was the gospel of grace preserved against Pelagius.

By the intricacies of theological polemics was the gospel of grace preserved against Erasmus.

By the intricacies of theological polemics was the gospel of grace preserved against Sadolet, Pighius, and Bolsec.

By the intricacies of theological polemics was the gospel of grace preserved against Arminius.

By the intricacies of theological polemics was the gospel of grace preserved against Heyns, Berkhof, Schilder, Holwerda, and Veenhof.

And by the intricacies of theological polemics will the gospel of grace be preserved against Shepherd, Gaffin, Barach, Lusk, Wilkins, Wilson, and all their hosts.

Theological polemics are necessary. When ministers and theologians will not engage in theological polemics, and when the people in the pew will not sit for theological polemics, heresy wins the day, and the truth of the gospel goes under.

Article 55 of the Reformed Church Order of Dordt charges all ministers and elders that "to ward off false doctrines and errors that multiply exceedingly through heretical writings," they must "use the means of teaching, of refutation or warning, and of admonition, as well in the ministry of the Word as in Christian teaching and family-visiting."[1] The same church order declares that the "office of the professors of theology is... to vindicate sound doctrine against heresies and errors."[2]

Upon professors, ministers, and elders who decline to engage in theological polemics, and upon the church members who encourage this dereliction of duty, when the gospel of grace and, thus, the church of Christ are threatened, falls the Lord's curse:

> Curse ye Meroz, said the angel of the LORD, curse ye bitterly the inhabitants thereof; because they came not to the help of the LORD, to the help of the LORD against the mighty (Judges 5:23).

Drawing the line from the federal vision to Jacob Arminius is correct and well-done. Still, it took years for a synod to nail him and his beliefs down. So it will take time for the Reformed churches to determine and condemn the federal vision.

This is not a question, calling for an answer. But it is an observation that allows for a comment.

From 1591—when Jacob Arminius exposed himself as heretical by preaching that Romans 7 is the confession of an unregenerated, unbelieving man, thus denying total depravity—to the Synod of Dordt, which condemned his theology as a false gospel, was a little less than thirty years. At least part of the reason for the delay of this condemnation of Arminian theology in the Reformed churches by the orthodox was the interference

---

1   Church Order of the Protestant Reformed Churches, Art. 55, in *Confessions and Church Order*, 397.

2   Church Order of the Protestant Reformed Churches, Art. 18, in ibid., 386.

of the state. The state would not allow the calling of a church assembly to judge the theology of Arminius.

From 1975—when Norman Shepherd's denial of justification by faith alone was known by the faculty of Westminster Seminary in Philadelphia, the board of the seminary, and the leading lights of the Orthodox Presbyterian Church, and soon thereafter by theologians in the Presbyterian Church in America and in other churches—to the present day is more than thirty years. The civil government has not hindered any ecclesiastical process of judgment and discipline.

During the past thirty-five years, and more, the Reformed and Presbyterian churches in which the false doctrine of the federal vision has appeared, whose ministers have taught the false doctrine openly and aggressively, and that have had to concern themselves with the false doctrine at the level of the major assemblies have not condemned the federal vision as a heresy and disciplined the teachers of the heresy. I refer to the Orthodox Presbyterian Church, the Presbyterian Church in America, and the United Reformed Churches. On the contrary, all three of these denominations have taken decisions at their major assemblies, whether general assembly, synod, presbytery, or classis, *exonerating* men who taught, and were charged with teaching, the theology of the federal vision publicly. Thus these denominations have officially approved the heresy.

The time taken by the orthodox Reformed in the late sixteenth century and early seventeenth century to condemn the theology of Arminius is no reason for hope that with more time the Reformed and Presbyterian churches in North America that are troubled by the theology of the federal vision will condemn the heresy.

First, the churches of our day have had more time to study and condemn the federal vision than the time it took the orthodox to condemn Arminianism in the days of Dordt. And the churches at the time of Dordt were hindered at every turn by the civil government.

Second, the churches of our day have the benefit of the Canons of Dordt and of the Westminster standards, which the

Reformed churches did not have in 1591 or in 1618–19. These creeds clearly expose and condemn the federal vision's doctrine of general, conditional, resistible, saving, covenant grace. These creeds clearly teach the gospel of sovereign, particular grace *in the covenant* that the federal vision denies. These creeds clearly teach justification by faith alone, apart from all the works of the justified, which doctrine the federal vision denies. Churches that have these documents as their creeds and that are committed to the Reformed faith these creeds plainly set forth would have taken only a couple of years to condemn and root out the theology of the federal vision—as long as it takes to discipline a stubborn heretic and to call and hold a general assembly or a synod.

Third, the churches of our day are so weakened by the prevalent doctrine of a conditional love and grace of God for all men in the preaching of the gospel—the well-meant offer of grace and the free offer (as it is popularly explained by hosts of ministers)—that there is neither inclination nor ability in the churches to condemn exactly this teaching, admittedly developed and emphasized, in the theology of the federal vision. How can ministers who preach, Sunday after Sunday, that the grace of God in the gospel and his sincere desire to save are wider than election condemn the teaching of the federal vision that God is gracious to all the baptized members of the visible, instituted church?

Fourth, the root of the theology of the federal vision is the doctrine of a gracious, conditional covenant of God with all the children of believers alike, that is, a doctrine of the covenant that cuts the covenant and its grace loose from God's unconditional election. If the churches themselves are not committed to this doctrine of the covenant, many of their ministers and theologians are. They may dislike the federal vision's development of this doctrine of the covenant. Some are distressed by one of the fruits now springing from the root, namely, denial of justification by faith alone. But they are determined not to take hold of the federal vision at its root. For the root is their own dear doctrine. So long as they maintain their doctrine of a gracious, conditional covenant with all the baptized children of believers alike, they will not condemn the federal vision. They cannot.

Time will not solve this problem.

Indeed, time is on the side of the federal vision. With every passing month, with every passing year, the leaven is permeating the whole lump.

From the perspective of the critic of the federal vision, what are the implications of dealing with the root of the error that others refuse to recognize? Why be a critic?

I am a critic of the federal vision because the federal vision criticizes, destructively, the Reformed faith, which I love. The Reformed faith, centering on justification by faith alone, is Scripture's gospel of grace.

I am a critic of the federal vision because I cannot stand by and allow the great work of Martin Luther and then of John Calvin, of the men of Dordt, of the fathers of the Secession, and of Herman Hoeksema to be overthrown.

I am a critic of the federal vision because men in no other denomination that I am aware of are able or willing to take hold of the heresy at its root, namely, the doctrine of a conditional covenant, which does not have its source in God's election.

I am a critic of the federal vision because I desire that members of the Protestant Reformed Churches appreciate the unique and precious heritage we have in the doctrine of the unconditional covenant; recognize the importance of the struggle in our history some sixty years ago on behalf of the unconditional covenant; take hold of the doctrine with renewed zeal; confess it boldly; and live it joyfully.

I am a critic of the federal vision because I hope that God may use my witness and that of the other ministers in the Protestant Reformed Churches to help men and women in other churches who are struggling against the federal vision, and to be of service to other churches in the purifying and developing of the grand doctrine of the covenant. Heresy often serves the advance of the truth.

If the response of other churches to our testimony to the truth of the doctrine of the unconditional covenant of grace is rejection, so be it. God uses the testimony to the truth also to leave men and churches without excuse. We speak, whether men hear or forbear. Christ does not call us to be successful. He calls us to contend earnestly for the faith once delivered to the saints (Jude 3).

What the Lord does with our witness is his business.

APPENDIX

HERETICAL THEOLOGY AND
A LACK OF LOVE

Hewitson's Trust and Obey*

The full-throated defense of Norman Shepherd and his theology by Ian A. Hewitson, *Trust and Obey*, appeared too late for me to take it into account in this book.

Nothing in *Trust and Obey* calls into question any aspect of *Federal Vision: Heresy at the Root's* condemnation of Shepherd's theology as heresy. On the contrary, *Trust and Obey* confirms the charge of this book that the theology of Norman Shepherd, which is essentially that of the federal vision, is heresy and that the root of the heresy is a false doctrine of the covenant of grace.

Because *Trust and Obey* is an avowed and ardent defense of the teachings of Norman Shepherd, it warrants critique as an appendix in the book.

The full title of the book is *Trust and Obey: Norman Shepherd and the Justification Controversy at Westminster Theological Seminary*.

Trust and Obey is composed of two parts. The first is a meticulous, merciless account of the mishandling of Professor Shepherd by the faculty of Westminster Seminary (Philadelphia), by the Board of Trustees of the seminary, and by the Philadelphia Presbytery of the Orthodox Presbyterian Church between 1974 and 1982.

---

* Ian A. Hewitson, *Trust and Obey: Norman Shepherd & the Justification Controversy at Westminster Theological Seminary* (Minneapolis, MN: NextStep Resources, 2011).

The second part is a vigorous apology for Shepherd's theology as orthodox. The author, Ian Hewitson, is a staunch defender of Shepherd and his theology. He is a critic of Shepherd's critics. Hewitson informs the reader that his book "will endeavor to show [that suspicion of Professor Shepherd] is entirely unjustified."[1] Hewitson's conclusion states:

> This book has sought to demonstrate that Westminster Seminary perpetrated an injustice against the Reverend Professor Norman Shepherd by inflicting upon him the severest of penalties: They removed him from his teaching position at the seminary. Part One demonstrates...that Westminster Seminary did not have adequate grounds to remove Shepherd...Part One allows for no other determination than that Shepherd was an orthodox Reformed theologian...The second part of this book demonstrates that Westminster Seminary also had no grounds theologically to remove him from his teaching post. Professor Shepherd's theological formulations concerning justification, baptism, election, and covenant were in harmony with Scripture and confession.[2]

The purpose of the book is to "remove suspicion from Shepherd and to restore to him that which is more precious to him than silver or gold—his good name, a name besmirched not by enemies of the gospel but by brothers."[3]

Hewitson's determination to defend Shepherd and to put Shepherd's theology in the best light possible makes this book all the more damning regarding the doctrine of Norman Shepherd. The heresy is not charged by a foe, but revealed, however unwillingly, by a friend.

---

1   Ian A. Hewitson, *Trust and Obey: Norman Shepherd & the Justification Controversy at Westminster Theological Seminary* (Minneapolis, MN: NextStep Resources, 2011), 16.

2   Ibid., 225.

3   Ibid., 226.

THEOLOGY OF A CONDITIONAL COVENANT

Shepherd's theology was the issue in the Shepherd "case," although "rhubarb" would be a more fitting term, because of the failure of his adversaries ever to make and prosecute a case, church politically. "At its heart, this struggle was over theology."[4] The theology that was the heart of the struggle was Shepherd's doctrine of the covenant. The Commission on Allegations that was to examine Shepherd's theology in light of criticisms of it stated that Shepherd made "the 'covenant dynamic' central in his theological work."[5] The first paragraph of that part of *Trust and Obey* dealing with Shepherd's theology raises the issue of "covenant, election, and baptism."[6]

The distinctive covenant doctrine of Shepherd that was the heart of the struggle was a doctrine of a *conditional* covenant.

> Throughout the controversy Shepherd maintained that a proper understanding of the relationships of divine sovereignty and human action to justification is to be found not in a further refinement of the *ordo salutis* [order of salvation] but in an appreciation of the structural significance of the covenant relation between God and man as that unfolds in the course of the history of redemption for an understanding of the application of redemption. For Shepherd it is the biblical concept of covenant that breaks through, and breaks down, the tension [*sic*] between faith and works in the doctrine of justification and that exhibits the proper relation between sovereign grace and human responsibility in terms of the functioning of the "covenant dynamic." The contours of Shepherd's suggested covenant structure of the doctrine of justification permit an alternative formulation to the traditional and sacrosanct "justification by faith alone"...*In short, the theological problem that provoked seven years of controversy*

4   Ibid., 220.
5   Ibid., 157.
6   Ibid., 105.

was how to speak of conditions in the application of redemption and yet maintain the priority of grace in the use of the word "faith." [7]

The quotation above is Hewitson's analysis of the Shepherd controversy. Shepherd's judges in the case that was never a case agreed that the heart of the struggle was Shepherd's doctrine of a conditional covenant. Reflecting particularly on Shepherd's teaching that all the branches of John 15:1–8 (a favorite passage of the federal vision) are alike savingly united to Jesus Christ, the Board of Trustees of Westminster Seminary said,

> The problem that is raised by the redefinition of our response in the New Covenant as essentially obedience is obvious. Coupled with Prof. Shepherd's emphasis on the non-hypothetical nature of N. T. warnings and the two-sided character of the covenant, *the conditional emphasis of the covenant dynamic is loud and clear.* [8]

All of Shepherd's heretical teachings arose from his doctrine of a conditional covenant of grace with all baptized members of the church alike, especially all the baptized babies of believing parents.

All of the teachings of Shepherd that a few of his colleagues on the faculty of Westminster called into question were rooted in his doctrine of a conditional covenant.

This is why neither the Westminster faculty, nor the Board of Trustees, nor the Philadelphia Presbytery of the Orthodox Presbyterian Church, nor the Commission on Allegations condemned Shepherd. This is the reason, *to this day,* none of Shepherd's critics, whether theologian or church, with one exception, has taken hold of Shepherd's heretical theology *at the root.* All share Shepherd's fundamental theological conviction, namely, that the covenant of grace is conditional. Some reject the bitter fruit; all approve the malignant root.

---

7   Ibid., 32; emphasis added.

8   Ibid., 180; emphasis added.

It was fitting that what finally did Shepherd in as a professor at Westminster (which was not the same as accomplishing his condemnation) was a series of lectures on "Life in Covenant with God."[9]

The failure of the authorities at Westminster Seminary and in the Orthodox Presbyterian Church to judge Shepherd's theology as false doctrine is scandalous. The failure cries to high heaven, where Jesus Christ sits on the throne of final judgment as king of his church, as dreadful dereliction of duty to defend the truth of the gospel of grace—the truth restored to the church at the Reformation and confessed in the Reformed creeds.

Shepherd's heresies were gross, grievous, and evident. Even though Shepherd was the typically subtle heretic and even though Hewitson exerts himself mightily to put the heresies in a good light, there is no difficulty in detecting Shepherd's heresies in *Trust and Obey.*

JUSTIFICATION BY WORKS

Shepherd denied justification by faith alone, that is, justification altogether apart from any and every good work of the believer, including the works he does by the sanctifying power of the Holy Spirit in his heart. Shepherd taught aspiring Presbyterian ministers at Westminster that justification is by faith and by the good works that faith performs. The struggle over Professor Shepherd commenced with the response of his students to questions at their presbytery examination concerning justification. The students responded that justification is by faith and works and that they learned this from Professor Shepherd.

> The event that placed Shepherd's teaching before the faculty was the refusal of the Orthodox Presbyterian Church to license David Cummings after he presented an understanding of justification that he believed he had been taught by Shepherd at Westminster Seminary.[10]

9   Ibid., 82.
10 Ibid., 39.

Shepherd taught that James 2:24, which states that justification is "by works...and not by faith only," speaks of justification in the same sense as does Paul in Romans 3:28, where the apostle affirms justification by faith, apart from works. That is, according to Shepherd, James 2:24 teaches that God's legal verdict of righteousness, declaring the guilty sinner innocent, takes the sinner's own good works into account. "The spark that ignited the powder keg in this controversy was Shepherd's exegesis of James 2:14–26."[11] Shepherd "believes both Paul and James are speaking of justification in the declarative sense...Faith and works might stand in parallel relationships to justification."[12] What "avails for justification" is "faith working by love."[13]

This explanation of James 2:24 and of justification, which has always been the Roman Catholic interpretation of James 2 and of justification, demanded that Shepherd harmonize James 2:24 with Romans 3:28, which obviously refers to justification as the legal verdict by the judge. Shepherd harmonized James 2 and Romans 3:28 by explaining "deeds of the law" in Romans 3:28 not as genuine good works, but as merely the ceremonial works required by the Old Testament or as only works performed with the motive of meriting. "Works of the law [in the 'Pauline letters' are] an external and formal adherence to selected legal prescriptions apart from faith."[14]

Shepherd, therefore, read Romans 3:28 this way: "Therefore we conclude that a man is justified by faith, without obedience to the ceremonial law and without works that do not proceed from faith, but not without good works that faith performs." This is to say, "A man is justified, in the sense of the legal verdict of God upon him, by faith and by the good works of faith." In Romans 3:28, Shepherd's Paul teaches that justification is by faith and by (genuine) good works.

11   Ibid., 221.
12   Ibid., 119.
13   Ibid., 124.
14   Ibid., 124.

Eight verses later, Shepherd's Paul, having forgotten what he had written in Romans 3:28, writes: "But to him that worketh not, but believeth on him that justifieth the ungodly, his faith is counted for righteousness" (Rom. 4:5).

Shepherd also denied justification by faith alone in his interpretation of Romans 2:13: "For not the hearers of the law are just before God, but the doers of the law shall be justified." Shepherd explained the text as describing what actually will, and must, be the case in the justification of the final judgment. Doers of the law will be justified, and they will be justified, not by faith alone, but by faith and by the good works of obedience to the law that faith performs. "Anything less than this [a working faith] is a dead faith and does not justify or save. That is why Paul can say that the doers of the law will be justified."[15]

Shepherd taught that "good works...are...necessary for salvation from eternal condemnation and therefore for justification." Although the righteousness of Jesus Christ is "the exclusive ground of the believer's justification...the personal godliness of the believer is also necessary for his justification."[16]

Shepherd's inclusion of the works of the sinner himself in the justifying act of God is condemned by the Reformed creeds (Heid. Cat., Q&A 59–64; Bel. Conf., Articles 22–24); contradicts Scripture in John 8:11 (the adulteress had no good work by which to be justified) and in Romans 4:5 ("to him that worketh not, but believeth"); overthrows the sixteenth-century Reformation of the church (which consisted mainly of the doctrine of justification by faith alone); and denies the heart of the gospel of grace.

Regarding this last, namely, Shepherd's denial of the heart of the gospel, Calvin's words to Cardinal Sadolet are applicable:

> You [Cardinal Sadolet, then, and the Rev. Shepherd, now], in the first place, touch upon justification by faith, the first and keenest subject of controversy between us. Is this a knotty and useless question? Wherever the

15 Ibid., 153
16 Ibid., 156.

knowledge of it is taken away, the glory of Christ is extinguished, religion abolished, the Church destroyed, and the hope of salvation utterly overthrown.[17]

Although this false doctrine, understandably, was on the foreground in the struggle at Westminster Seminary and in the Orthodox Presbyterian Church between 1974 and 1982, it was by no means the only doctrine of the gospel that Shepherd corrupted. How could it be? Justification by faith alone is, as Calvin described it, "the main hinge on which religion turns."[18] Shepherd's bending of the hinge was the ruin of the entire Christian religion according to the Reformed understanding of it.

CHANGEABLE PREDESTINATION

Shepherd denied biblical predestination, as confessed by the first head of doctrine of the Canons of Dordt. He taught that election in the New Testament is not an eternal, unchangeable decree, but a temporal, mutable decision of God. Specifically, Shepherd taught that election in Ephesians 1:4 is not the "eternal decree of God." Rather, "Paul speaks from the perspective of observable covenant reality and concludes from the visible faith and sanctity of the Ephesians that they are the elect of God."[19]

Ephesians 1:4 reads: "According as he [God] hath chosen us before the foundation of the world, that we should be holy and without blame before him." Verse 5 sheds more light on the eternal election of verse 4: "In love having predestinated us unto the adoption of children by Jesus Christ to himself, according to the good pleasure of his will."

In Shepherd's theology, Ephesians 1:4 is the apostle's conclusion concerning all the members of the Ephesian congregation, that they are the elect of God. And all of them are the elect of God, *for the time being.* However, according to Shepherd,

---

17 John Calvin, "Reply by John Calvin to Letter by Cardinal Sadolet to the Senate and People of Geneva," in *Tracts Relating to the Reformation*, trans. Henry Beveridge, 3 vols. (Edinburgh: Calvin Translation Society, 1844), 1:41.

18 Calvin, *Institutes*, 3.11.1, 1:726.

19 Hewitson, *Trust and Obey*, 185.

"some [of the 'elect' of Ephesians 1:4] may fall away" and become reprobates. "Paul warns against that possibility. Were some to fall away, he would no longer speak of them as the elect of God."[20]

Judas Iscariot was an elect, in the sense of Ephesians 1:4, who later is "rejected [reprobated] as a son of perdition because of his apostasy."[21]

Accompanying the radical revision of the Reformed doctrine of election, as confessed in the Canons of Dordt, 1.7 ("Election is the unchangeable purpose of God"), was a novel doctrine of reprobation. "Reprobation" in the theology of Norman Shepherd "is not incontrovertible."[22] That is, reprobation is not the eternal, decisive, unchangeable appointment of a certain number of persons to perdition.

Shepherd's revision of creedal predestination was rooted in his covenant doctrine. He said so. "The election of God is reflected upon from the perspective of covenant."[23] "Reprobation from within the context of the covenant...is not incontrovertible."[24]

In the purportedly biblical and Reformed theology of Norman Shepherd, predestination is controlled by a conditional covenant. If one trusts and obeys, God elects him. If this believer fails to perform the conditions of the covenant, as is a real possibility, God changes his election of the man into a reprobation of him. If the lapsed elect repents and again performs the conditions of the covenant, he regains his status as the object of election. One can only hope that his final breath finds him performing the conditions of the covenant. This must be the wish of God as well for those in whom he has begun salvation.

What is this wretched doctrine but the application of the conditional predestination of Arminianism to the covenant and covenant salvation?

20 Ibid., 185.
21 Ibid., 183.
22 Ibid., 181.
23 Ibid., 184–85.
24 Ibid., 181.

Election—the eternal, sovereign, gracious, unchangeable decree of God of Ephesians 1:4 and of the Canons of Dordt, 1.7—does not govern the covenant and the salvation of sinners in the covenant. Rather, Shepherd's covenant—the conditional contract or relationship between God and every baptized person, which depends upon the sinful member of the covenant—governs God's election.

Shepherd's protest that he still also acknowledges an eternal decree of God is worthless. It is mere deception and foolery. For, first, this eternal election does not amount to anything. It does not do anything. It does not govern the covenant, the covenant Christ, and covenant salvation. The only election that is involved in the covenant—*the covenant of grace!*—is Shepherd's "covenant election," and this is a weak, changeable, and pitiful thing. The eternal decree, to which Shepherd pays lip service, is, in Shepherd's theology, inoperative. It is a dead letter.

Second, there is no biblical basis for the eternal decree in the theology of Shepherd. If Ephesians 1:4, which explicitly states that God chose some "before the foundation of the world," does not refer to the eternal decree, *no* passage of Scripture teaches it. The only basis of an eternal decree of election is the word of Norman Shepherd that, in spite of his consignment of it to the realm of the insignificant, there is such a decree. The word of Norman Shepherd is not sufficient to establish doctrine.

Did any one of the many judges of Shepherd's doctrine of election ever point out to him that the Canons of Dordt, 1.7 makes Ephesians 1:4–6 the biblical ground of election not as a temporal, changeable, "covenant" election, but as "the unchangeable purpose of God, whereby, before the foundation of the world, he hath, out of mere grace, according to the sovereign good pleasure of his own will, chosen, from the whole human race…a certain number of persons to redemption in Christ…"?[25]

---

25   Canons of Dordt, 1.7, in *Creeds of Christendom*, 3:582.

UNIVERSAL ATONEMENT

Such is the intimate relation both of justification and the cross and of election and the cross that error concerning justification and concerning election must also extend to the doctrine of the atonement. Shepherd taught heresy concerning the atonement of the cross of Christ.

Shepherd criticized Calvinism for denying that the world of John 3:16 includes all humans without exception. By this denial "the Calvinist...hedges on the extent of the world [in John 3:16]." The trouble with the Calvinist is that he explains the world of John 3:16 "in terms of the doctrine of election." Contrary to Calvinism's limitation of the humans included in the world of John 3:16 to the elect, Shepherd declared that the word "mean[s] exactly what [it] says." What it says in Shepherd's thinking he made plain when he immediately added, "The Reformed evangelist can and must say on the basis of John 3:16, Christ died to save you."[26]

Shepherd meant that the Reformed evangelist may rightly say, "Christ died for you," to every human. It is the evangelist who may say this. Evangelists address people outside the church— the unbaptized and unbelieving. That Shepherd meant that the evangelist can and must say "Christ died for you" to every human without exception, he made explicit in his book, *The Call of Grace*: "The Reformed evangelist can and must preach to everyone on the basis of John 3:16, 'Christ died to save you.'"[27]

Unless Shepherd thought that Reformed evangelists are liars, he taught that Christ died for all humans without exception and that he died for all, because God loved all humans with the saving love of John 3:16.

Hewitson's conclusion regarding Shepherd's doctrine of the atonement defies not only logic and rationality, but also the plain meaning of words. Having quoted Shepherd as denying Calvinism's limitation of the extent of the atonement to the elect and as declaring that an evangelist can and must say to

26 Hewitson, *Trust and Obey*, 208.
27 Shepherd, *Call of Grace*, 84–85.

every human "Christ died for you," Hewitson concludes that "Shepherd affirms the doctrine of definite atonement... [Shepherd's] teaching 'does not challenge' the doctrine of election or the doctrine of definite atonement."[28]

One may not insult a Presbyterian doctor of theology by attributing to him ignorance of the fact that by "definite atonement" the Reformed faith understands that Christ did not die for all humans without exception, but only for the elect. It is inconceivable that Dr. Hewitson does not know that the Reformed faith has expressed its doctrine of definite atonement in the ecumenical creed, the Canons of Dordt.

> For this was the sovereign counsel and most gracious will and purpose of God the Father, that the quickening and saving efficacy of the most precious death of his Son should extend to all the elect, for bestowing upon them alone the gift of justifying faith, thereby to bring them infallibly to salvation: that is, it was the will of God, that Christ by the blood of the cross, whereby he confirmed the new covenant, should effectually redeem out of every people, tribe, nation, and language, all those, and those only, who were from eternity chosen to salvation, and given to him by the Father; that he should confer upon them faith, which, together with all the other saving gifts of the Holy Spirit, he purchased for them by his death.[29]

No Reformed evangelist "can and must," or may, say to every human whom he meets, whether on the streets of Philadelphia or in the wilds of Brazil, "Christ died for you." No apostle of Christ ever conducted missions in this way, according to the book of Acts.

Hewitson's affirmation that Shepherd taught definite atonement, therefore, must be the deliberate use of an orthodox

---

28   Ibid., 208.

29   Canons of Dordt, 2.8, in *Creeds of Christendom*, 3:587.

phrase to express an entirely different, unorthodox meaning. It plays the reader for a fool.

Shepherd taught universal atonement. He taught an ineffectual atonement. Many to whom his evangelist said "Christ died for you," evidently because Christ did die for them, nevertheless perish in hell.

The Reformed faith repudiates with all its heart such a view of the cross of the eternal Son of God in human flesh. In the cross of Christ, the Reformed faith glories.

RESISTIBLE (SAVING) GRACE

As is evident from Shepherd's doctrine of a conditional justification, an inefficacious, changeable election, and a cross that fails to save many for whom Christ died, Shepherd denied sovereign grace. This is the necessary implication of his doctrine of a conditional covenant, which is the root of all his theology. The denial of sovereign, irresistible grace was glaringly evident in Shepherd's doctrine of salvation—the regeneration, sanctification, and perseverance of sinners.

Working with John 15:1–8, Jesus' teaching about the vine, the branches, and the necessity of bearing fruit, Shepherd taught that God saves all who are baptized with water by uniting them all alike, savingly, into Jesus Christ. This is the sovereign work of grace. Whether those united to Christ, and saved, remain in Christ and enjoy everlasting salvation, however, depends upon their performing the condition of bearing fruit. Some fail to perform the condition and are separated from Christ, so that they perish everlastingly.

Shepherd rejected the explanation of John 15:1–8 that distinguishes "between two kinds of branches" and that holds that "some branches are not really in Christ in a saving way." He criticized the concern that the passage be "squared with the doctrines of election and the perseverance of the saints."[30]

Thus Shepherd rejected the explanation and criticized the concern of John Calvin. Commenting on John 15:1–8, Calvin

---

30 Hewitson, *Trust and Obey*, 178.

wrote, "Can any one who is ingrafted into Christ be without fruit? I answer, many are supposed to be *in the vine*, according to the opinion of men, who actually have no root *in the vine*." Calvin added, "Not that it ever happens that any one of the elect is *dried up*, but because there are many hypocrites who, in outward appearance, flourish and are green for a time, but who afterwards, when they ought to yield fruit, show the very opposite of that which the Lord expects and demands from his people."[31]

Hewitson defends Shepherd's explanation of the passage:

> Shepherd contends for grace sovereignly bestowed (the first part of the covenant) [the uniting of all the baptized into Christ] and for the necessity of faith and repentance (the second part of the covenant) [the dependence of remaining in Christ and obtaining everlasting life upon the performance of conditions].[32]

This is not a doctrine of sovereign grace. Sovereign grace not only begins the work of salvation in the sinner, but also maintains and perfects it. Sovereign grace not only unites the dead sinner to Christ, but also causes the now living sinner to produce fruit and in this way to persevere in Christ unto everlasting life.

Grace that begins the work of salvation, but fails to perfect this work—fails to bring it to its end in the resurrection of the body—because the saved sinner fails to perform the condition upon which the perfection of grace depends, is resistible grace.

Shepherd's covenant grace is the resistible and losable grace of Arminian theology that the Canons of Dordt reject as an aspect of the Arminian heresy, when the Canons reject the error of those "who teach that the true believers and regenerate not only can fall from justifying faith and likewise from grace and salvation wholly and to the end, but indeed often do fall from this and are lost forever. For this conception makes powerless

---

31   John Calvin, *Commentary on the Gospel according to John*, trans. William Pringle, (Grand Rapids, MI: Eerdmans, 1949), 2:108, 110.

32   Ibid., 196.

the grace, justification, regeneration, and continued keeping by Christ, contrary to" many passages of Scripture, which the Canons then quote.[33]

Hewitson, like Shepherd himself, muddies the waters by denying that Shepherd's conditions, upon which grace and salvation depend, are "meritorious." "Shepherd teaches that there are conditions of the covenant and...he teaches these conditions are not meritorious."[34]

It makes not a particle of difference whether the conditions are meritorious or nonmeritorious. What is heretical is the teaching that God's saving grace in Christ is ineffectual, fails to accomplish the final salvation of one in whom it began salvation, and is dependent upon conditions that sinners must perform. Both Rome's meritorious conditions and Shepherd's nonmeritorious conditions rob God of his glory in salvation and give the glory to the sinner who performs the conditions.

A THEOLOGY OF DOUBT

Inherent in a doctrine of salvation that denies the sovereignty of grace is the real possibility of the falling away of saints and, therefore, also the loss of assurance of salvation. Shepherd's theology is a theology of doubt and fear. Some who are united to Christ and begin to enjoy the blessings of salvation, including justification and eternal life, and, therefore, who possess faith, for justification is by faith, can and do fall away from Christ and perish eternally. Some branches, which are as savingly united to the vine as those that bear fruit and abide in the vine, fail to perform the condition of bearing fruit, are cut off from the vine, and are burned.

No one, therefore, who believes in Jesus Christ and begins to enjoy eternal life is, or can be, certain of abiding in Christ and inheriting eternal life in the day of Christ.

All believers must live in the supreme terror that they might fall away from Christ and go lost forever.

33 Canons of Dordt, 5, Rejection of Errors 3, in *Confessions and Church Order*, 177.
34 Hewitson, *Trust and Obey*, 195.

The theology of Norman Shepherd gives assurance to those who believe and practice this theology that they are saved at the present moment. Because this assurance is based on their own performing of conditions rather than on the eternal, gracious, unchangeable election of God through faith in Christ crucified, this assurance is a false assurance.

In the theology of Norman Shepherd, one may have the assurance that he will be saved in the future, even everlastingly, *if he continues to perform the conditions. But he does not have the assurance that he will believe and obey to the end.* For in the covenant theology of Shepherd, believing and obeying are conditions that the sinner must perform. They are not the working of sovereign grace in the sinner, flowing to him from the gracious election of God, merited for him by the cross of Christ, and irresistibly maintained in him by the Spirit.

Assurance in Shepherd's theology is the conditional and, therefore, highly uncertain assurance of Roman Catholic and of Arminian theologies. It is not the assurance of the Reformed faith, as expressed in the fifth head of the Canons of Dordt.

> Of this preservation of the elect to salvation, and of their perseverance in the faith, true believers for themselves may and do obtain assurance according to the measure of their faith, whereby they arrive at the certain persuasion that they ever will continue true and living members of the Church; and that they experience forgiveness of sins, and will at last inherit eternal life.[35]

The alleged assurance of the theology of Shepherd is, in reality, doubt.

SHEPHERD AND DORDT

The theology of Norman Shepherd is heresy.

It is the heresy exposed and condemned by the Canons of Dordt.

Shepherd and Hewitson do not rescue Shepherd's theology from Dordt's condemnation by calling it a *"covenant* theology": temporal, changeable *covenant* election; universal, ineffectual

---

35 Canons of Dordt, 5.9, in *Creeds of Christendom*, 3:594.

covenant atonement; resistible, losable *covenant* grace; the falling away of *covenant* saints; lifelong, terrifying *covenant* doubt.

Dordt's doctrines refer to and describe the *covenant* gospel—*covenant* election, a *covenant* cross, *covenant* grace, *covenant* preservation, and *covenant* assurance.

How did the pernicious notion ever gain entrance into Reformed and Presbyterian churches that the Canons of Dordt apply to some saving work of God other than his covenant of grace? Where did the evil idea originate that Dordt is describing some gospel other than the gospel of the covenant of grace? Who gave currency to the foolish thought that Dordt condemned all theologies of a universal, resistible, saving grace of God—a grace that does not have its source in and is not governed by election—*except such a theology of the covenant?*

There *is* no other gospel than the gospel of the covenant of grace.

There is no other salvation than the salvation of the covenant Jesus Christ.

Everything Dordt teaches, it teaches about the covenant. The theology of Dordt is covenant theology.

And the theology that Dordt condemned in 1618–19 was a false, heretical theology of the covenant. Arminian theology was covenant theology, as Arminius and his disciples declared, loudly and clearly.

A Reformed or Presbyterian theologian, or layman, for that matter, would have to be blind not to see that the theology of Norman Shepherd is, essentially, *in all respects*, from a conditional predestination to the falling away of elected saints, the same conditional covenant theology that the Synod of Dordt condemned. He would have to be blind not to see that Shepherd's theology opposes the same gospel of sovereign, particular grace that the Arminians fought so fiercely in the late sixteenth and early seventeenth centuries.

But the majority of the faculty at Westminster Seminary, the majority of the Board of Trustees of the seminary, a blue-ribbon Commission on Allegations, and the Philadelphia Presbytery of the Orthodox Presbyterian Church could not see this. "Professor Shepherd was exonerated three times by the Westminster faculty, twice by the Board of Trustees, and by his own presbytery—exonerations that have never been rescinded."[36] "In the end, the Commission [on Allegations] exonerated Shepherd...(even though no charges were extant)."[37] Not one of these bodies—the judges in the quasi-case—ever condemned Shepherd's theology during all the seven years of the Shepherd controversy at Westminster.

LACK OF LOVE

This brings up part one of Ian Hewitson's important defense of Norman Shepherd—the handling of the Shepherd controversy between 1974 and 1982.

The treatment of Shepherd and his teachings by adversaries and supporters alike was appalling.

On the part of Shepherd's adversaries, their dealing with a colleague, one whom they were called to view and treat as a brother in Christ, was a travesty of justice and a trampling upon the basic rules of Reformed church order. They called into question Shepherd's orthodoxy, *in the fundamental matter of justification*, without ever making a formal charge of false doctrine, complete with grounds, and then processing this charge before the appropriate church assemblies.

The result was seven years of high-level theological debate and bitter doctrinal wrangling, as though the issue were merely academic, and, in the end, the dismissal from his teaching position of a man who, not only had never been condemned for heresy, but also had never been charged.

But there is far more to the result than only this, bad as this is. The result was also that Shepherd's theology has never been condemned at Westminster Seminary or in the Orthodox Presbyterian Church. On the contrary, on every occasion that his theology came to the attention of some body of judges at Westminster or in the Orthodox Presbyterian Church, Shepherd's teachings were approved. His defenders on the faculty

36 Hewitson, *Trust and Obey*, 16.

37 Ibid., 222.

and in the Orthodox Presbyterian Church, of whom there were many, were perfectly within their rights to continue teaching the theology of Norman Shepherd. And they did. Shepherd was gone; his theology remained.

In addition, the result of the failure to deal with a suspected heretic according to the Reformed church order, which in this aspect is the rule of Christ in Matthew 18:15–18, was that Shepherd and his theology were loosed upon the conservative Reformed and Presbyterian churches in North America, indeed upon the Reformed churches worldwide. He left Westminster Seminary and the Orthodox Presbyterian Church with "clean papers," as the Dutch Reformed say, that is, as an orthodox theologian and as a good Christian man, indeed a good Christian man much abused by foes. This good reputation enabled him to spread his theology abroad as the federal vision. Those who did not charge him with heresy, and then press the charge, if necessary to the general assembly of the Orthodox Presbyterian Church, bear responsibility.

There is also a personal side to the mishandling of Shepherd. Christian discipline always has as its purpose the repentance and salvation of the sinner. This purpose applies also to the discipline of theologians and professors of theology. Heresy is a sin. The heretic is a sinner. The Church Order of Dordt mentions heresy first in its list of "gross sins" that render a minister worthy of deposition from office and excommunication.[38] Shepherd's adversaries, who correctly saw that he was guilty of heresy regarding justification, were duty-bound to exercise church discipline in order, if God willed it, to bring Professor Shepherd, their brother, to repentance and salvation. The keys of the kingdom have this power. Theological fighting for seven years does not.

No one ever brought a charge against Professor Shepherd, according to Hewitson's careful account of all the proceedings in the Shepherd controversy. The adversaries only raised

---

38   Church Order of the Protestant Reformed Churches, Art. 80, in *Confessions and Church Order*, 402.

questions, deadly serious questions, about the orthodoxy of Shepherd's teachings, over a period of seven years. The Board of Trustees, as well as the Philadelphia Presbytery of the Orthodox Presbyterian Church, allowed this to continue. And then the board of Westminster Seminary permitted this disorderly conduct to be successful in the ouster of Professor Shepherd from the seminary.

Appalling as this aspect of the handling of the Shepherd case is, there is another aspect that is still more appalling. In the providence of God, despite the absence of any formal charge, the theology of Shepherd came to the attention of the faculty of Westminster Seminary, to the attention of the Board of Trustees, to the attention of the Philadelphia Presbytery of the Orthodox Presbyterian Church, and to the attention of a high-powered panel of Reformed and Presbyterian theologians and churchmen—the Commission on Allegations.

Shepherd's theology came to the attention of all these bodies and men for judgment.

They examined Shepherd's theology thoroughly, under the heavy pressure of trouble in the seminary and in the church.

They tested Shepherd's theology, in a way, for seven years.

These were some of the most learned and respected men in all of Presbyterian Christendom.

All the bodies and a majority of the men approved Shepherd's theology as Reformed orthodoxy and "exonerated" Shepherd.

This was a theology that taught justification by faith and by works; the election of Ephesians 1:4 as conditional and, therefore, changeable; the atonement of Christ for all men without exception; saving (covenant) grace that is resistible and losable, not infallibly bringing to glory; and the falling away from Christ, grace, and salvation of (covenant) saints.

Hewitson implicitly accuses Shepherd's adversaries of a lack of love for Norman Shepherd. That was reprehensible.

Far worse was the lack of love for the truth of the gospel on the part of Shepherd's defenders. Lack of love for the truth of the gospel of grace is the fast track of apostasy in these last days (2 Thess. 2:10).

INDEXES

INDEX OF NAMES

INDEX OF SCRIPTURE

INDEX OF CREEDS

OTHER WORKS BY THE AUTHOR

In addition to writing *Federal Vision: Heresy at the Root*, David J. Engelsma has authored and coauthored numerous other books, written countless articles for the *Standard Bearer* magazine, and penned several pamphlets pertaining to Christian life.

RFPA PUBLICATIONS WRITTEN BY DAVID J. ENGELSMA

Better to Marry: Sex and Marriage in 1 Corinthians 6 and 7
Bound to Join: Letters on Church Membership
Common Grace Revisited: A Response to Richard J. Mouw's
　He Shines in All That's Fair
Covenant and Election in the Reformed Tradition
The Covenant of God and the Children of Believers:
　Sovereign Grace in the Covenant
Hyper-Calvinism and the Call of the Gospel: An Examination
　of the "Well-Meant Offer" of the Gospel
Marriage, the Mystery of Christ and the Church:
　The Covenant-Bond in Scripture and History
Prosperous Wicked and Plagued Saints: An Exposition of Psalm 73
Reformed Education: The Christian School as Demand of
　the Covenant
The Reformed Faith of John Calvin: The Institutes in Summary
Reformed Worship *(coauthor with Barrett Gritters and
　Charles Terpstra)*
Trinity and Covenant: God as Holy Family
Unfolding Covenant History: Judges and Ruth

RFPA PUBLICATIONS EDITED BY DAVID J. ENGELSMA

Always Reforming
Communion with God: Reformed Spirituality
Peace for the Troubled Heart: Reformed Spirituality
Righteous by Faith Alone: A Devotional Commentary on Romans
The Sixteenth-Century Reformation of the Church

Visit the RFPA website, www.rfpa.org